February 8th

How we lost our Homeland

Jeron North

The true story of a German girl in World War II

Author: Jeron North
Cover design: Jeron North
ISBN-13: 9781500818302
ISBN-10: 1500818305
Contact: readmorebooks101@gmail.com

February 8th

Contents

This book is dedicated to Artur and Klara Maiwald and the almost 17 million people who lost their homes through flight and expulsion from 1944-1950.

2 million of them did not survive.

Preface

Is it worthwhile to sit down many years after it all happened and write a book about my childhood in Silesia, the eastern part of Germany? Have not all the traces been erased after so many years, is my memory still good enough? Who would be interested in my past, my adventures and thoughts today?

These questions I kept asking myself before I made notes for this book trying to find the answers. Even while writing, these questions came up again and again which made the whole process difficult at times. Sometimes I didn't write a word for months but then again a lot in a few days when I could hardly stop. I relived my early years in a manner I never believed possible.

Never before had I thought about writing a book and certainly not about myself until my son repeatedly asked me to. He said it was important to him and after the countless books I have read, the time had come to tell my own story. I began to collect facts and memories and gave them to my son so he could turn them into a book. Maybe I don't need to answer the above questions. Perhaps the book had only to be written to deal with my past and to understand some of the meanings of life, my life? Again there were questions and doubts.

And yet, dear reader, the book was written maybe because not all questions have one or more answers. I have no reason to hide and do and say what others expect of me. My memories were so vivid that after a difficult start I felt a certain satisfaction that pushed me forward. Like many others I have seen the worst sides of life especially at a young age and often thought that my existence would certainly come to an early end. I grew up in a time of political madness and tragic impasse and I hoped it would never happen to anyone else and yet it still does today. Can't we learn from the past?

My thoughts are with all the lovely people I met along the way who became victims of time, everybody who helped me to believe in myself, all those who gave me something to eat when I had nothing left and all those who gave me shelter when I had none. May they all rest in peace; I shall never ever forget them.

Very special thanks to our parents. We could always rely on them, they loved us children unconditionally, more than their own lives and no task was too much for them. I survived the darkest chapter only because of them. From the bottom of my heart I wish them only the best on the other side and that they can finally be united in eternal peace.

With infinite love and gratitude

Ingeborg Maiwald

-1-

The Village

The tannery is closed and all business activities are over and done. It has become quiet in the factory where the employees did their work. The big steam generator is dismantled. It had always fulfilled its task, day after day for so many years. With it, a long chapter of our family came to an end and I would like to tell you our story from the beginning as I experienced it.

Glockschütz was a very small German village near the city of Breslau (now Wroclaw, Poland) in Silesia and the two hundred inhabitants were simple people, as they were found in any other village. The majority of the population lived mainly from agriculture as there were many open fields and pastures around. Glockschütz had no places of interest and you would rarely find a stranger there. There were no shops and if you needed something, you had to go to the village of Hundsfeld or modern Breslau. Some inhabitants carried their trays to the bakery in Hundsfeld if they had no oven at home to bake their bread. Before my time the houses were not always locked when no one was at home, but a broom in front of the door indicated that no one was around and you could see that from afar. There were no crimes and robberies were unheard of. We had electricity, which could not be claimed by all the villages in the area. A telephone could not be found in every house, but we had one in the office which was necessary for the business.

My father's birthplace in Glockschütz

At this place in the Trebnitz District, I was born Ingeborg Gertrud Marta Maiwald on Thursday, March 1st, 1934 and I was the second daughter of Artur and Klara. The first daughter was Ruth, the third one was Ursula. As it was common at that time I came into this world at my parents' house. The memories of my birthplace are still very vivid. I can particularly remember the little kitchen, where a separate water pump was installed on the wall. It had a foot long wooden handle that had to be reciprocated and the water then flowed through a pipe about ten centimeters in diameter into a basin. Having a pump in the house was by no means a common thing, but a pleasant exception. In bad weather we did not have to go into the courtyard to fetch water. We had wallpaper in each room and timber floors which always seemed to shine. From the ground floor a straight wooden staircase led upstairs and beneath it was a small storage room. We had no bathroom so the children had a zinc tub in the kitchen and our parents had a shower at the factory. The house was not very big, but it was enough for a small family and for my parents it was a modest, solid start. Almost every house in the village had a vegetable garden whereas we had fruits of many kinds and work had to be done there on a daily basis. Fresh food was stored in the basement for a short time since we had no refrigerator. There was an outhouse behind our house and Dad took me there in the dark, when I just had to go. A toilet in the house was very rare at that time.

Our father Artur was a slightly stocky, strong man with dark brown straight hair. I think I can say that he was a handsome man with even facial features and a melodious voice. He always made the decisions and set a good example; he was certainly highly respected by his workers. He is best described as quiet, thoughtful and fair in all his ways. Dad had an opportunity in his early childhood to show that he was a born leader. At the time of the First World War the older boys played imaginary war campaigns in the woods and did not take little Artur with them. One day one of the boys dropped out and they needed a replacement. They asked Artur if he would like to join in as private. The nine-year-old only replied, "If I can't be general I'm not coming!" They made him general. For me he was the greatest, because he could simply fix anything. Our mother Klara was a slender, pretty woman with dark brown, almost black hair and she was very good at organizing. She always worked hard and did not ask for much. On Sundays, she would put on her best dress and freshly shined shoes before we went to church together. She always put great emphasis on honesty; she could not stand liars and lazy people. In the evenings everything had to be clean and orderly, otherwise there was trouble, that's where the fun ended. I'm not saying that she was strict; she only wanted to teach us good discipline. In fact, she was very generous and shared everything, especially with us children and we loved her for it. Both parents were non smoking, which was perhaps an exception in those days.

Dad's parents were Paul and Pauline Maiwald. They operated a small tannery in Glockschütz. Paul's father used to be a furrier with his own business. I never knew my great-grandfather's name.

Dad was only fourteen years old when, in 1919, he lost his father from the effects of a spillage in the First World War. Regrettably there was no money available for an autopsy, because if it had not been for the consequences of war, the cost would have to be carried by our grandmother Pauline. So she received no war pension, which would have been very small anyway. Re-marriage seemed to be the only way out, especially since she wanted her son Otto to take over the small tannery. She had managed the business by herself until Otto got married.

Factory workers 1912. Pauline with son Otto on the right.

Mum's parents were Emil and Klara Löffel. Out of eight siblings she was the first to be engaged and was twenty-two years old when she married Dad, then twenty-four, in February 1929. Emil Löffel died on July 13th, 1915 during the First World War as a result of a cholera epidemic in Belverne, France. The news of his death came late on October 16th, 1916, yet his body was never found. There was even a great-grandmother named Auguste Puffke and she sometimes minded my sister Ruth. Once, Ruth almost tripped into the manure pit, as my great-grandmother came running just in time to catch her. Auguste fell badly and broke her thigh. She died a short time later at a hospital in Breslau.

My big sister Ruth was born on April 16th, 1929. Until her fifth birthday, she stayed with Grandma Klara and her still unmarried children at her place in Klein-Bischwitz during the week.

The house in Glockschütz was built after the tannery was completed and there was no suitable place for the little Ruth. Every Saturday she was collected by Daddy and taken to Glockschütz as the house was finished. Mum was always involved in the business and could not take care of her. The relatives in Klein-Bischwitz loved Ruth very much, for she was the first grandchild and truly the center of attention! Ruth was slim and had black, slightly wavy hair.

When I came along we both had our beds in the parents' bedroom, where my children's bed was made out of steel tubes and a fine metal mesh on the sides. My grandmother Pauline used to gently rock me to sleep until one night when I said, 'Stop rocking, I want to sleep...!'

Once when I had whooping cough, I was sleeping between my parents, with my mum watching over me when I had a fit. We didn't have the drugs that are available today and it was very serious. The next day I got some drops from our family doctor, but they did not help significantly, yet somehow after a few days I was better again.

In the spring of 1925 my father borrowed 3,000 Reichsmarks from a man by the name of von Schweinichen. He was the richest man in the area and he did not require any collateral. The banks would not give a loan and Dad founded his own tannery in Glockschütz on the first of May at the age of only nineteen. The financial conditions improved only after the economic crisis in 1929. Pauline's sons made good progress with their tanning businesses. Dad and Uncle Otto received enough orders from the Breslau furriers and Dad was excellently suited to make and invest money.

Our family occupied only the ground floor of this house in Glockschütz. Uncle Paul and Aunt Trude, my mother's sister, were living upstairs in a small apartment. Trude was my favourite aunt because she made the best pies and cakes and I was happiest, when she gave me a taste of her butter cream directly into my mouth. The pleasure was simply unbeatable! She had a bit of spare time, when she was in the house and every now and again I would check into her apartment to find out when the next cake was in progress. Everyone else was busy so I could always be the first to taste it.

Ingeborg and Aunt Emma

We had enough to eat during this time, so we were able to take a girl in during school holidays each year. Her name was Irmgard Reiter and she happened to be Ruth's age. She slept on the couch in Dad's office and put her few clothes in an office closet space. Every new season our parents used to buy us children dresses from a department store in Breslau, named Brenninkmeijer. It goes without saying that Irmgard was also dressed by our parents.

There was a cordial friendship among us, we knew she had only a mother as a parent. She came from a big city and was part of a government program that sent children and young people on holidays to the countryside, where the food was much better. That was called *Kinderlandverschickung*.

My parents owned the tannery and employed a few good workers. During the day, Mum worked there and a maid named Lisbeth did the housework and was responsible for us children. Grandma Pauline took care of me during the day. She lived a couple of houses away from us and went back home after she had put me to bed in the evening.

In the afternoons the two of us went for a walk sometimes. We took a blanket and spread it out in one of our nearby meadows. Then my grandma told me stories and I listened intently. She seemed to know the answers to my questions about all sorts of things and so we had a great time together. She taught me a lot in those days, always in a patient manner. I especially remember the story of a burning child she had rescued from the flames of a farmer's house and she did not want that to happen to me. The child had probably been playing with matches and had been left alone in the kitchen without supervision. That story was so intense that I stayed away from matches for a long time. On Sundays after lunch, we used to drive with our parents to Breslau to the "Scala" cinema and we watched fairy tale movies and movies with Shirley Temple, Judy Garland, Laurel and Hardy, etc. The names of the actors I learned later, but I do remember what the cinema looked like: the chairs and walls were covered with red velvet, the curtain was made of the same fabric and the floor had a thick red wall-to-wall carpet. It was always a great adventure for us and we looked around until the lights went out and the show started. We wanted to see who else was there so maybe we could talk about the movie to someone the next day, but that never happened. The other villagers had no cars, and probably not the money for the trips. I never noticed that anyone would envy me, but today I'm sure some did. My reality did not necessarily coincide with the reality of other children who had to settle for less. I did not realize at first that we grew up in a privileged family. I enjoyed those times and I always looked forward to Dad opening the door of his car and letting us in. We did not always know where we would go, of course, that only increased our excitement and we tried to guess where our destination would be. The rides were entertaining for us and we had a lot of fun. Sometimes our dad asked us to settle down so he could concentrate on his driving. We brought balloons from the Breslau amusement park back into the car and there we sat in the back seat holding them in our hands. Maybe we fooled around with them and distracted Daddy, at some point he rolled down the window and suddenly my balloon found its way out. I was sad and the otherwise nice trip came to an abrupt end for me. A little consolation was found the next morning, when I saw Ruth's balloon sitting small and lifeless in the corner.

Another trip had to be cancelled because Dad had a painful renal colic; he took us home and then he drove to the hospital all by himself! He brought the removed kidney stones back and showed them to us.

In addition to the car we had a beautiful horse drawn carriage with large spoke wheels that we used on sunny days.

In the first half of the 1930's Dad bought the run-down estate No. 110 in the village of Heidau from the Laudien family. At that time the only animals left were about 10 to 15 sheep feeding on undeveloped arable land. Our family continued to reside in Glockschütz, while Grandma Pauline and her husband Hans Krause moved to Heidau. Mum's brother Karl and his wife Trude moved with them and together they lived in the house that later became our home. Dad often went to Heidau to oversee the construction of a new tannery right opposite the house.

The Maiwald family in 1937

My most important early memory is the birth of my sister Ursula on October 23rd, 1937. I was three and a half years old and had blonde medium length hair. Ruth and I were awakened that night by our parents and brought to Grandma Klara's in Klein-Bischwitz. I went back to sleep in my grandmother's big bed. We called her Muttel like everyone else. Muttel's bed was made of wood and had all four bedposts topped with large wooden balls. I thought that was great and imagined they were four knights who guarded me while I was sleeping. The bed of my parents did not have those balls, even though it was made in the same period. Later it became a children's bed in Heidau, which I shared with Ruth. Our parents then acquired a modern bed made from light birch. Ursula was born and I was excited about having a little sister and was already making plans what I would play with her when she was a little bigger. It was something new and exciting for me, because I was not the smallest in the family anymore and had some experience to share with my younger sister. But I had to wait for quite some time...

Muttel and family

Aunt Frieda sometimes minded us kids and I remember that the phone rang once and she never went to answer it. She was not accustomed to a telephone, because Klein-Bischwitz had none. I thought it was strange but funny.

-2-

The Move and the Yellow Stars

In 1937 our maid Lisbeth Kiewitz and I went to a store in the town of Wendelborn in order to buy a wreath for the Corpus Christi procession. I had to sit on the luggage rack of the bicycle and away we went. The road surface was not as good as they usually are today and I was glad when we finally arrived. To our disappointment, there were no more wreaths left and so we had to come up with something else, since we did not want to return home empty-handed. Lisbeth suggested that we could pick flowers by the wayside, and make a wreath with daisies. That's what we did and we were very proud of the result. We rode back to Heidau, placed the wreath into a large dish with water overnight and it was fresh but wet the next morning.

The procession took place in the village of Hundsfeld, and went without incident. I liked the music and watched many people who attended the event in their best clothes. Events like that were infrequent and so it was a nice experience for me. Unfortunately, I was at the beginning of an illness and I got increasingly worse. I fought bravely for most of the time, but then I had to give in and my parents put me back into the car. We drove home and I went straight to bed. Grandma Pauline was notified and consulted, to find out which cure would promise the most success. She was well educated in those things and I felt better soon. As I mentioned before, she was great to play with. In summer we used to go to a well in the woods and made soap bubbles in the sunlight. Grandma would always make the big ones and with her help I was able to make them just as big after a while.

Heidau (now Golanka Dolna) was a small village about fifty kilometers west of Breslau and had about six hundred and forty inhabitants. Our new property there was larger than the one in Glockschütz and should cater for the new requirements. Dad had big plans for the future and he wanted to put them into reality as soon as possible. The old factory had become too small. The house belonged to a farm in Heidau with land as far as I could see. When we made the first car trips to Heidau Dad gave me the junk mail which came in envelopes. I opened them and looked at the pictures until I was so dizzy that I once had to vomit into the glove compartment. However, this was neither the matter of bad images nor the driving; it was the combination of both. Dad remained calm and cleaned up everything when we arrived. Before we left for Breslau, he always took the mail to the post office and cheques to the Eichborn Bank. I usually waited in the car and later, when we were already living in Heidau, I saw people with a yellow star on their chests on the square in front of the bank. I did not understand the significance of the stars back then. Much later I learned that it was a must for Jews to wear this marking.

I was also allowed in the riding arena, where Dad took riding lessons. Once it was terribly cold, as I stood on a balcony and watched the horsemen and of course Dad. I also wanted to become a good rider so I watched everything with excitement. The coach gave the instructions, and everybody in the group was doing their best. You could see the breath of the horses as they made it up and down the arena doing figures. After an hour it was over and we went back to the car. We had a catalytic heater in the car, but it could not save me. I came home with a cold and Mum scolded much with Dad for taking me. A freezing cold indoor arena was not the right place for a four-year-old, she said.

One Saturday our parents prepared the upcoming move to Heidau. The workers from Glockschütz knew they would lose their jobs because the way to the new tannery was too far for them. Some of them were Dad's former school buddies and they protested by leaving a note with the following wording on a pile of wet calf skins, 'You can nail the skins yourself (stretching to dry)!' Mum and Dad nailed the skins to the frames, which was no easy work, especially for a woman.

In 1938 we finally moved to Heidau. Uncle Karl, Aunt Trude, and their daughter Sigrid, who all lived there until our arrival at the new house, moved back to Gross-Bischwitz. Karl had taken care of the farm during Dad's absence. The Laudien family, the former owners, lived on the ground floor, my grandmother Pauline lived in the right wing. The house was much bigger than the old one, had a wide entrance with stairs and a porch near the kitchen entrance. As customary, the whole house had a basement.

Our home in Heidau

When we moved in, the Laudien's had left the house and had moved to Berlin, as we learned later. They were broke and had to sell the property. What they did in Berlin, I do not know. Dad purchased new animals soon after. We had cows, horses, pigs, chickens, turkeys and geese. There were also our two dogs, with whom I often played and considered them to be loyal friends. One was Dad's hunting dog called Minka and the other one was called Strolch. Anyway, we had lots of animals and I always found something to do. We had twenty-two dairy cows, four oxen and eight horses, including four beautiful horses, of whom I still know the names of the two best ones: Bolko and Hellebarde. They were Dad's competition horses and he won some prizes with them. Those two horses I wanted to ride later as well and every few weeks I had to measure myself to see, if I was finally big enough. Where should I get the patience?

Dad had a few cars and he started out with a three-wheeler called Tempo, around 1925. With this car he collected the goods for the tannery. There were skins of foxes, rabbits, Persian lambs, minks as well as chemicals to be shipped. The customers were furrier shops in Breslau. Later, he had a white Audi with a black top, but we drove with a larger car from Glockschütz to the cinema, which must have been about 1936 or 37, maybe it was an Opel Admiral. In Heidau we had two trucks. They were being used for raw skins, chemicals, salt and fuel from the train station and finished goods taken back to the station. There was a petrol station in Parchwitz (now Prochowice) owned by Mr. Kupsch and we paid with ration tickets there. The distance between Heidau and Parchwitz was three kilometers. Two green DKW cars with revolver gear shifts were there and we also had a black Wanderer car which was only allowed because it had been converted to wood gas. One truck also ran on wood gas, and each of the trucks had a trailer. In addition there was a tractor and a caterpillar for field work.

We had a second farm in the neighbouring village of Dahme. Dad bought it two years after the property in Heidau and it belonged to my sister Ruth. There was the same amount of cows and horses and also a tractor. The beautiful house was very big and looked like a small castle, but I have not been there many times. Taken together, there were two hundred hectares of land. During the war, farmers were required to keep a certain amount of cows because the milk yield was heavily regulated. Germany needed milk, and every farmer had to do his best to reach the quota and to keep the animals healthy. Dad did not want to have as many dairy cows as they ate almost the whole produce of the fields. The rates in agriculture were regulated by the government.

There were pigs to be fed and many had to be given away because of another government regulation. They were counted officially; it never went without strictest checks and lists. Once a month the milk inspector came to us. Each cow had a blackboard on its stand in the barn with their names and dates of birth and birth of calves, and fat content of the milk. The number written on our milk cans was 1194.

Next to the gateway to the village street on the left hand side was the ramp where the so-called "schweizer" put the milk cans on a very large cart where they were collected by the milk truck each morning. A "schweizer" was in charge of the milk production.

My life in Heidau had a good start. Sometimes I sat on a blanket on the kitchen floor and played with clothespins first. After that I turned the kitchen chairs upside down and climbed over them. Grandma Pauline took care of me and I loved her above all else. She probably knew a lot about children, because I lacked nothing. As primitive as my toys were, I was never bored with them. Pauline had married retired postal official Hans Krause, an Upper Silesian. She had a very special relationship of trust with my mother and from her I know that she deeply regretted that marriage.

One of the pastures stretched from the factory down to the Weide Creek, a tributary of the mighty Oder River, so we had sufficient space for our games. Our parents planted many young fruit trees which bloomed in the spring. One year there was a huge flood in the meadows, and since it was summer the water was warm and I was wading around in it with the children from the neighbourhood. Most of them were the sons and daughters of our factory workers, and we all had a lot of fun and something to talk about after. One boy's name was Dietmar and he was the son of Wilhelm Schär, a reliable man who worked in the tannery with ten other Glockschütz employees until September 1939. Then they all got drafted into the military. After Wilhelm was gone we never heard of him again.

When pigs were slaughtered children were not allowed to watch, but I know that venison was processed into the salami. That way we had a couple of sausages more and they contained less fat. Every Saturday Uncle Otto came to visit us from Glockschütz for hunting or fishing. Dad had both, a little forest and a piece of the Cat Creek. Sunday morning when our maid Angela used to make dumplings from boiled potatoes for lunch, Uncle Otto prepared his bait. He rolled little balls, which he then put into a square tin box with a lid. Otto took the fish he caught home at night. Fish was not on the menu in our family due to the bones. Dad once had swallowed a fishbone as a child and nearly choked to death.

Sometimes Uncle Otto brought his two best workers and friends, two Slovenian brothers, who worked at his tannery due to the war in Germany. In the evening they made music with Ruth's accordion and their own guitars in the lounge room, which also served as an office. Ruth had been taking violin lessons in Glockschütz, but unfortunately there was no music teacher in Heidau. It was a shame because I think she would have become a good musician. On such nights we were allowed to stay a little longer and listen. I thought that was very nice, although I no longer remember what music they played. For us it was a welcome change and that was good enough.

In Heidau we had a World War I veteran as a night watchman. He lived on the first floor of the workers' building. His name was Mr. Hornig and he had a sick wife; we children paid her a visit sometimes. When he retired, there was a new watchman from Liegnitz (now Legnice) from a security and surveillance company and he arrived every afternoon by bus. He had to punch his card at the clock several times during the night and then went back home the following morning. He was not the only security guard and he was replaced after a few months. There must have been a rotation system in place so that the men did not become too complacent.

As previously mentioned, my parents bought our clothes in Breslau at Brenninkmeijer's, a very large department store. The most exciting things for me, however, were the escalators and elevators. I went up and down all by myself until I was admonished. Dad used to pick the clothes for us children, Ruth always got the colours red, I got the blue ones, Ursula was too young and when she was bigger, there was nothing left to buy and no more department stores. At that time we had a seamstress named Miss Käthel from Liegnitz, living with us in Heidau for a few weeks. She was practically a member of the family. She was not married, a little older and had only a mother as a parent in Liegnitz.

In my early days we had beautiful wooden building sets, dolls, doll carriages, a post office game with many cards and letters with envelopes. I got some old forms and outlines of the sticky-backed stamp sheets from our office, so the game was more authentic. A puppet theater was very popular, and Dad was often the puppeteer and played from text books.

'Kasper, I've come to get you,' said the Devil, and Kasper asked back, 'What, you've got a hole in your shoe?'

In Glockschütz the Laterna Magica was something special. It was similar to a slide projector but with a strip, projecting the whole story onto the wall. We watched fairy tales, and perhaps also the first Walt Disney stories. Around 1938 we had a movie projector in Heidau, that was only operated by Dad on Sundays and public holidays. There were, unfortunately, only eight different films. On some Sundays Dad collected a few children after church, brought them home and then there was a screening for all of us. There was no cinema in Heidau, and so we just had our entertainment at home. The last movie was, 'The Leader at the Ober-Salzberg.' Dad had to buy a copy, for he was a businessman and it was unwise not having one. The film was kept on a shelf in the office. Other businessmen did just the same.

On Sundays we went to the pictures in Parchwitz without our parents. The children's shows started at two o'clock. Sometimes we walked and on other occasions we took the bikes. There was very little traffic and we were safe.

My first vehicle was a blue "wipproller", a kind of scooter that ran best when one jumped on it with a little speed and began to rock a pedal with one foot. It gave me much pleasure, and after a short learning curve I got really good at it. My grandmother Pauline used to keep my wipproller hidden when my knees were bruised. Once I found it after days of searching in the smoke chamber on the top floor of our house. As soon as the wounds were healed, the wipproller was back in action.

At the age of five I got Ruth's girls bike and I learned to ride it by going always around a walled manure pile. Ruth got a new bike, for she was already ten years old, and kept it for the following years. Our parents also had bikes and we rode along the streets and lanes in summer, which I always enjoyed very much, particularly because I was able to show how good I was riding my little bike. Even Grandma Pauline had one. Every Friday she rode her bike to Parchwitz and went shopping. She brought newspapers and new magazines for Dad and herself. I do not know why exactly the magazines were bound in thick books by her. Whenever someone was ill and had to stay in bed, he or she received such a book on request. We children copied the front pages and transferred them onto graph paper, after which they were then filled with coloured pencils. More often than not there were portraits of film stars. Tracing was strictly forbidden by our grandmother. The books had to be kept clean and any damage was out of the question.

Grandmother Pauline

-3-

The School and the Rocking Horse

In the summer of 1939, Dad was drafted by the Wehrmacht (Armed Forces) and underwent several weeks of basic training. He had no choice, it was general duty. In September, the war started and then Dad had to join the troops in the Polish campaign as a driver of a captain. Our car, an Opel Admiral, was taken by the Wehrmacht and repainted in army gray. Dad practically had to drive in his own car to the front. He did not like it at all; and of course, he was never compensated for it. After two weeks my father came back unharmed and without a shot fired. However, the car was kept by the military forces. Dad was exempted from fighting and any military duties because his tannery was appointed as a war-supporting plant and from then on he had to tan rabbit furs, which were then used as lining for leather jackets for the ground staff of the Luftwaffe (German Air Force). The Opel remained in the possession of the captain, who got a new driver and then was driven in France. The story of our car ended there as it ran over a mine one day and there were no survivors.

All our male workers were drafted by now and Dad hired Polish workers who came voluntarily to Germany seeking work. They found employment in factories and agriculture. Dad always treated them well and had their families staying with them. Several houses were quickly built on our property, thus creating new living space for them. A total of one hundred and eighty people were working in the factory.

We also had some goats, which had the advantage that their milk was not taken from us by the government. From the first year of the war onwards the goat milk was given to the Polish families. The women also kept many rabbits in rabbit-hutches next to the houses.

The Maiwald family in 1942

After Easter in 1940, I went to primary school and I still remember the first day. I was excited! The school was not too far and Mum took me there, then Grandma Pauline filled this task. I did not want to go all by myself, since Ruth's class began earlier and I knew no other kid my age in our street. Then luckily Gisel Just (pronounced "yoost") came into the picture. I had seen her once before at our place, when she had come along with her father and asked my dad, 'Excuse me please, may I ride on the rocking horse for a while?'

I was completely stunned by so much politeness coming from this girl. The Just family lived at the Pirl Estate near ours and from that day on we were best of friends. The rocking horse was the jewel in our house, no doubt. I loved it. It was one of a kind and did not operate like a rocking chair but more like a swing. The horse had a sturdy timber frame with a suspended solid board, where the horse's legs were attached. Horse and board became one unit and made it possible to be moved back and forth. The movement was close to a real horse. It was the size of a foal and covered with genuine calf skin, mane and tail were made from real horse hair, and the eyes were made of glass. It had a genuine bridle, a saddle made of leather and I can say without exaggeration that I have never seen such a beautiful rocking horse again. If I still had it today I would find an adequate place in my house for it. This leaves only the memories and it is unfortunate that we have no photos today.

I always did my homework at the big table in Dad's office and when I finished I sometimes tried to copy different fonts, which I found in magazines. I only had a pencil and my work did not quite turn out as good as I wanted, however, in the end I was rather satisfied. Once I was given beautiful pens with nibs and ink by Mr. Schulze from Leipzig as a gift. I felt like an adult for the first time, or at least as a teenager. That was pretty much the same for me back then. I did not have a fountain pen, but I could hardly wait to get one. Dad said I was too young for it.

Only in the dead of winter we played inside the house; otherwise the whole village was our playground since the beginning of my school days. Before that, the games were limited to the yard; I could build my own little world in the garden and I was happy. The grass beds were edged with white stones; the gravel paths were so beautifully done that I could play there with my doll carriage. In addition, there was a swing made from green steel tubes with a wooden seat.

In the first week of school smart Gisel turned up with a beautiful little hat, but then she left it at home. Maybe it was too cute for her. We had no uniforms at school and the students were dressed as well as their parents could afford to. From day one we were sitting on a bench next to each other and soon became inseparable. It must have been so obvious that even our teacher Mr. Lang called us Max and Moritz, two well-known German characters from a book by Wilhelm Busch, but we never knew which one of us was Max and which one was Moritz. Unfortunately he was only a year with us because he was drafted too. Our pranks were not planned; they most probably happened unconsciously. We would understand each other perfectly, and we could always rely on one another. Actual damage was never done, except that I once got a spanking from Mum, because we vexed Erna Sekulsky to the limit on the way home from school. Erna was an only child and daughter of an employee of my father's. Anyway, Gisel and I ran after her and spun the lock around on her school bag, which she carried on her back. She resented that of course. That really got us going and we then spun it even more until she finally ran home crying. As one can imagine, she immediately told her mother about it, who told Mum the next day. Mum spanked me without any further discussion or hesitation. Gisel was lucky and got nothing from home; it had not been passed on to her parents. Yet another time I've drawn Mum's anger and got spanked again. With a bunch of children I did not go into our own strawberry garden, but climbed over the fence and we ate the best strawberries Jungfer's garden had to offer. We were caught by their maid Maria, and in no time the news travelled to Mum's ears. The afternoon was over for me. I really had such a black and blue behind that even Grandma Pauline said, 'Say Klara, did you have to hit her so hard?'

We school children were encouraged by the teachers to collect everything recyclable and bring it to school. There was a room in which things like paper, rags, metal and even animal bones and teeth were stored until collected.

Barrel running was a popular sport. We picked up big empty barrels from the tannery and jumped on them with bare feet and then we had races. The barrels had a diameter of nearly a meter and one had to walk backwards, so that the barrel moved forward. On a smooth floor, it's easier; we had a hard-packed dirt floor and every step you had to be ready for anything. Running too close to the dung heap was not very popular. Nobody was injured in the process and therefore it was not forbidden. In retrospect, I think it was good skill training for the things that were to come. One had to concentrate, to balance, and to observe the co-combatant and jump off at the right moment without getting injured. Only a few years later I was confronted with tasks that these skills demanded. But then it was no longer a game.....

We also played hide-and-seek like the older children. The children were divided into two groups and we wore coloured wool ribbons around the wrists to determine the group we belonged to. Our version of the game was to conquer the ribbons of the other team and who had the most was the winner. I think, the game was never fully resolved and when the evening came we all went home without a whimper because we were hungry and had to be with our families before dark. We did have fun anyway, and on another day we played it again.

In the summer we rode our bikes or walked on foot almost every day to the public swimming pool in Parchwitz. First, we took swimming lessons and had professional supervision. Gisel got her certificate in the first year being eight years old, I got mine a year later with nine. To get the certificate we had to swim fifteen minutes in one go, without touching the pool edge. The swimming lessons did cost five marks, which was a lot of money. We were privileged, for most children could not do the course because their parents did not have enough money or maybe they thought it was superfluous. Ruth once overheard the grandmother of a schoolmate saying to a friend, 'Get this, Jockel paid for the cinema tickets for the rich Ruth Maiwald!'

Ruth was fifteen or sixteen years old at the time. She said she never thought of paying because the boys always paid for the girls. I only want to say that it never occurred to us that we were privileged, even though our parents owned a factory, real estate and cars. In the eyes of the villagers we were somewhat "better."

A dangerous game was walking on cross beams in the barns. The barns at the Pirl Estate as well as ours had high cross beams, where we were playing catch. I was not comfortable at first and I got all my courage together, for I did not want to be laughed at as a coward. We were five meters high, it was very dangerous and I cannot remember who came up with this idea. Either way, we played up there and unknowingly put our lives at risk. In our barn, where the finished rabbit furs were stored, there was a rack where we could easily climb to the high beams. All five children were up in the air and the game had started, when my father suddenly appeared in the barn and calmly said, 'Come down slowly, it's too dangerous.' Today I can say with full admiration, he defused the whole situation with calmness and superiority and brought us all safely back to the ground. That was unique and his self-control was one of his best traits. Since that day we never went up there again, our consciousness had changed forever.

Instead, we formed a theater group, and practiced with different actors. We wanted to invite other children to watch and we even manufactured our own tickets. Everything should be as genuine as possible. Unfortunately, we did not have the right cardboard or a print shop, so we used strips of paper, put them into the sewing machine and let the needle perforate the paper without a thread. We were really proud. A swing was attached to a beam in the barn and we invented tricks to do for one or two children. We had trouble with the curtain, because the sheets we had were not big enough. Finally, the whole project had to be cancelled, because our maid Angela discovered the arrows that I had put up as guides for the audience. They pointed up to the first floor where the hay was kept and where we wanted to perform. Angela said the first floor was too dangerous, because there was no handrail. We could not play on the barn floor due to lack of space. During the summer months we had dinner on the veranda, which I liked a lot. There was fresh sweet strawberry milk and sandwiches. I loved the butter spread on so thick that it left bite marks behind. I did not particularly like the stewed liver sausage that we often had during the war, but I ate it because of the circumstances; there was not much choice. I also did not like barley soup, which was so gray and unsightly. Otherwise I ate anything, especially in bad times, when our hunger left us ravenous. It was always good when I was home for dinner. Grandma did not like it very much when we went for a swim every day and so I had to outsmart her sometimes. I put on my bathing suit under my dress, and disappeared for the afternoon, and then I came back with my hair still wet, when all were already seated at the table. 'The chlorinated water is a curse, child,' said Grandma.

Grandma kept things in order; I can tell you that much. After lunch, we had to have a quiet snooze and before that we went up to Grandma, waiting for us kids at the top of the stairs and everyone got an egg yolk, mixed with sugar. Now and then she would beat egg whites, which we liked better. Some time later, Ruth was exempt from the eggs since she was already a commercial apprentice in the office and worked with Marianne Köhler. The sisters Ursula and Marianne worked alternately for us. Marianne was first called by the government for Labour Service, then she came back and Ursula had to go to do the same. So we had Marianne at the end. She had a bright head on her shoulders and she taught a classmate fractions. I had brought both of them home from Upper Heidau one day. The two were originally from the city of Frechen near Cologne, and had left their hometown because of all the alarms and therefore they had little possibilities for a proper education.

My sister Ursula grew slower than I expected. With her I had hoped for a playmate. As it is common, most children do not have much patience and so it was with me, too. I did not play that much with Ursula at that time, she had a nanny and was still too small. I would much rather go with my older sister, but a five-year age difference was again too much for Ruth. She did not need to take me along when she went off with her group of friends. In addition, in the summer months she was allowed to go to the pictures at 5pm on Sundays, while I had to be happy with the 2pm show. Only once she had to take me and my friends: Ruth was in the Parchwitz public pool with her classmates when a thunderstorm approached and the area had to be closed. The swimming guard let us through the exit gate and there she saw a group of teenagers gathered on bicycles. After a brief, 'Where to?', she asked the boys from Ruth's group to take us on their bikes and bring us home. The boys took us without hesitation and we all made it safely back to Heidau.

The solidarity among us sisters was limited, however, if someone had dared inflict harm on one of us, we would have no doubt held together, through thick and thin. This situation did not arise until then, we knew each other well and everyone had their group of friends.

At the Heidau School I had an extraordinary position, which I actually did not want. Our teacher was allowed to collect the class with the older students in the fall and come to our field where my father had kept a particular spot of potatoes untouched so that the teacher had food in winter. He and the students only needed to just pick them up. I did not need to pick peas either, but would have been happy to go there with the other children and help. Instead I had to keep an eighth-grader under supervision when I was only in my fifth year. He had to stay back after class because he had not done his homework. He did not seem to be very intelligent, but I do not want to misjudge him, because it is likely that he had to work on his family's farm and therefore had no time for studying and doing homework.

Every now and again I brought something home to my parents. Once I had silkworms for parachute silk and I placed them onto brown paper on the grand piano. Every day I plucked mulberry leaves after school and put them on the silkworms. Another time it was even a small family. Grandmother, mother and a two-year-old girl from a West German city were supposed to move into a house with an old woman, but the place was in such a bad state it left them speechless. Me too.

As school children we had to take German evacuees to the appointed addresses in the village. They came from the cities where food was scarce. Finally I decided to take them home and from then on they lived upstairs in a guest room. I cannot recall that there was a surprised look at home. I knew my parents would not refuse shelter since they were always helpful and had raised us to be likewise.

Ursula Köhler gave me her roller skates from her childhood as a gift, and I practiced on the few paved roads in the village. We all had ice skates, too, or rather, steel blades we would strap under our boots. Ruth was the only one with proper white skates, which she got from Uncle Ferdinand, who had to serve in France as a soldier. She and I had each a pair of skis, but unfortunately there was no mountain in Heidau and so we could only do some cross country skiing. The mountain called Hirseberg, was too far away and only good enough for a sled, which was also great fun. The winter afternoons were always very short and we had to leave early, in order to be home before dark. The roads were not lit, even in the village, there was no street lighting. Dark meant really dark. Most of the time we were freezing, despite warm underwear and knitted woolen stockings. When we returned home we vigorously walked around in the kitchen to warm our feet on the tiled floor. After that we took a hot foot bath in a zinc tub, and then we had dinner with the parents.

We children were a strain to our house maids, especially my sister Ruth. Once she was late for school. The maids immediately jumped around her, everything had to be done very quickly. Ruth had the math problems explained by Dad while he was still in bed, then she had breakfast, while Maria braided her hair and Lucie cleaned the shoes and dressed her. That very moment her school friends turned up and were waiting in the kitchen. Finally, Ruth was finished at the last minute and together they made their way to school.

One day I accidentally overheard a conversation between two girls at the post office, which somewhat puzzled me. They called my two sisters princesses, Ruth was Sleeping Beauty and Ursula was Snow White. My name was not mentioned in this context...

Ruth was in a classroom that consisted of the grades 5 to 8, and class started at eight o'clock, whereas mine started at ten minutes to nine. Because of the war, classes were put together into one classroom. At our primary school, grades 1 and 2 were taught in one room, grades 3 and 4 in another one. Our teacher, Miss Mantell, was an officer's daughter and every morning she came with her motorcycle from Liegnitz. Later on, she stayed in Heidau when there was no fuel available anymore. Mr. Kretschmer taught the grades 5 to 8. The head teacher Otto Kretschmer was the father of the later highly decorated naval officer Otto Kretschmer, Jr. (Lieutenant Commander, Knight's Cross with swords and diamonds) and the fighter pilot Joachim Kretschmer, who thundered several times with his plane deep over the schoolyard before the war, while Ruth and her class had a break. He was shot down only a few months after the war had started and was killed. His brother became and still is the most successful U-boat commander in history and was awarded several times. Ruth and I never shared a classroom which might have been a great deal of fun...

In Heidau there was a farm named Staude, and in 1941 the barn was set on fire by the owner who then ended up in jail. He was broke and did not know what to do. Dad bought the farm at the auction and created new housing for the Polish workers of his company. I saw the fire in the middle of the night. The flames flared up very high and I was awakened by the noise of the volunteers who tried to extinguish the fire.

Later, in 1942, Czechs were employed in Dahme, our second estate, including a woman called Wladislawa Pollock and her two daughters who were a few years older than Ruth. Wally was twenty-three and Nelly twenty-one. Mrs. Pollock turned to Dad and asked him to give Nelly a job at the house, for she had a weak heart and could not do hard labour in the fields. I heard my parents talking about it and they decided to take all three of them to Heidau. They lived on the top floor, where we had two maid's rooms and two guest rooms. They moved into one of the guest rooms, the other one was for Uncle Otto on the weekends.

Mrs. Pollock worked with Mum in the finishing department of the tannery, where all rabbit furs were checked, and if necessary, re-worked. Sometimes the fur was not perfect and had to be straightened with steel combs. The whole department was under Mum's supervision and there were about fifteen to twenty women working. Wally was a trained seamstress and from then on, we no longer needed Miss Käthel. Nelly knitted for us while being kept on the books, but she never had to work as hard as the others. She made very nice things for us and we liked all three of them very much.

When Uncle Otto, Dad's brother, came one Sunday to go fishing again he told Dad that a former school friend of my father's was in trouble for his only workhorse had died. There were no other horses to purchase; on top of things he did not have the money anyway. Dad did not hesitate and told Otto he would take care of it. The following Saturday one of our horses was taken from the stable and Dad drove it to his friend. He left it there as a present.

It was still 1942. As children, we had no aprons like the other children who had to put them on after school. We did not even have white aprons for Sundays, as it was common in our time. We had enough clothes to last for the whole week. The weekly washing was done in the hall outside the kitchen. First, it was soaked and rubbed with soap. During the war, Grandma Pauline even made soap over an open coal fire in the yard. She used scraps of flesh from the tannery, and added a little Eau de Cologne to improve the smell. Ursula and I had our hair washed with egg yolk and rinsed with vinegar water.

On a few Sundays I went fishing with Uncle Otto and I even caught a fish once. I was surprised and proud at the same time. I got a little dirty but that was no problem. We had a solid Miele washing machine and an electric winch that was attached to it. That way one could squeeze the wet laundry. The laundry was then hung to dry under the roof. The house maids had to carry the baskets of wet clothes up three flights, where they were also pressed with a hot iron. In summer, the clotheslines in the garden were used, which were located along the fence. On the other side the chickens had their outlet. The geese pen was on one side of the house and the animals were taken to the paddock in the morning, where one could also find the obstacle course for Dad's horses. Since the beginning of the war, he did not practice there anymore. I think that he missed that very much, although he did not talk about it in our presence. He was very passionate about his horses and riding was his favourite hobby. The war changed everything. Dad was the best horseman I ever saw and I loved him for it. He used to listen to the nightly news on the radio. It was not a German broadcast, but it was the BBC London in German language. That was prohibited of course and he always had to be careful not to get caught by government officials.

-4-

Uncle Paul and the Radio

Sometimes there was a little dispute between my parents because of Mum's relatives in Klein-Bischwitz. She even hid my doll that I had gotten there one day, so Dad would not see it. It was an old story that occurred in many families, and still occurs today. Mum's brothers did not like Artur and they said to her before the wedding, 'What do you want with someone who only has big ideas in his head? You'll see you won't get very far with him!' They were probably a little jealous.

Only Uncle Paul and Aunt Trude were loyal to my parents and were often invited to come to Heidau. Paul worked in a factory called Borsig as a train driver and did not get drafted. I went twice to Klein-Bischwitz on holidays, when I was eight and nine years of age. Trude and Paul picked me up in Heidau and Dad took us to the train station in Jeschkendorf. From there we took the train to Breslau where we found their bicycles locked up at the station. I sat behind my uncle and my luggage was strapped to my aunt's bike. That's how we travelled to Klein-Bischwitz. Trude and Paul helped during the harvest since all the men were drafted by the Wehrmacht. When Paul arrived after work with his bicycle, he had dinner and then went out again to prepare food for the animals. He mowed the grass with a scythe, loaded it onto a horse-drawn carriage, the horse's name was Hans, and drove back home. This sounds all too easy today, but it was hard work and it was very time consuming.

I joined him and gave him a hand with the loading as much as I could and it was already dark when we arrived back home. The horse was taken into the stable and looked after, and then we washed our hands and went into the house. Paul put himself right in front of the battery-powered radio and started tinkering with it. The whole village had not yet been connected to the mains,

43

although there was an Air Force airfield not too far from Klein-Bischwitz. At last the first sounds came from the speaker, then we could hear some of the messages, the reception was really bad. The most exciting thing for me, however, was watching (grandmother) Muttel and my aunties as they sat around the dinner table with dimmed lights. One by one they bowed their heads to one side because they were exhausted from the farm work. I developed a game and had bets with myself, who most likely was next to fall asleep. Paul saw what I was doing, smiled and worked the radio again. For the adults it was necessary to know what was going on, because everyone hoped the war would soon be over and we could return to normality. How little we knew what lay ahead of us....

At home in Heidau we children always had an early night unless there was a special occasion. We went to bed after dinner which we had at seven o'clock in summer and at six o'clock in winter. One can imagine that I enjoyed my time in Klein-Bischwitz. I was allowed to stay up to ten o'clock, even though I was tired too, of course, but watching adults falling asleep was just too interesting to be missed and a welcome change. There were also a few children around to play with. I particularly remember Erika, who was Ruth's girlfriend and lived in a small house with a thatched roof. She was truly a wild one and we often did some crazy things around the farm. Despite the holidays, I had to write a page each day with calligraphy in an exercise-book with double lines. When it was full, I rode the bike to Aunt Lowak in Gross-Bischwitz, who owned a mum-and-pop shop, and there I bought a new book without presenting the old one, because I had to show my work to the teacher after the holidays. In any other case we had to take the old books for recycling before we could buy a new one. When the time had come to show the teacher he had forgotten all about it and I didn't need to show it at all. Quite disappointing. After a week Trude and Paul went back home to Glockschütz where Trude was now in charge of the farm since the eldest brother Josef had been drafted by the Wehrmacht. She took care of everything on the farm.

In earlier years my grandmother Pauline did not get along well with her mother-in-law, in whose house she lived. Pauline used to be a good looking and graceful young woman and she was sent to collect the money from the furriers in Breslau. It was all about getting the bills paid in full. She also worked in the tannery, and she told the family that when she went to bed the night was over in no time. She asked her husband to wake her when he woke up in the middle of the night so she would realize she could go back to sleep. Another time I did hear her saying that she had gone hungry quite often as a child and would therefore put a piece of bread under her bed on a good day which turned stale and then eat it on a bad day. Her father went to work in the morning and sometimes he brought back two fish at night. He ate one; the other one was shared amongst the family. During a diphtheria epidemic her sister passed away, only she and Aunt Christine survived. Pauline married Paul Maiwald at nineteen and Christine married Paul's brother Otto at seventeen. Both men were in the First World War; Paul came home and lay in a coma for a long time before he died in 1919. His brother lost his life in the war and Aunt Christine was now a widow with her only son Paul, who then died in the Second World War. With her second husband Robert Arlt she had four children. Two sons fell in the Second World War, their daughter Friedel died at the age of eighteen to a severe inflammation. Their little son was five years old, when he played with other children on a garbage heap, where he found a pack of tablets. He swallowed them and was beyond saving. Robert and Christine were still looking for relatives after the war, and indeed found a grandson in the German Democratic Republic, whom they visited a few times.

-5-

The Concentration Camp and the Babushkas

Somewhere it is written: "To save a man is to save the whole world." For this I remember the following story: Two Polish workers one day came to our father and told him about their problem. A friend named Karol had been collected by the police and sent to prison. He was alleged to have threatened his employer with a pitchfork. Before he was taken away, he said to Dad that he was looking for a new job. Karol was a two-meter man and Dad could have used him well for a certain job in the tannery. He was arrested soon after and went to prison. It did not take long and he was taken to a concentration camp. I can not remember how Dad did it and how he explained it to the officer in charge that he needed this strong man for his company. As an eight-year-old I knew nothing about procedures, it was not openly talked about, especially not in front of children. In any case, one morning Dad went to Poland and returned with Karol in the evening. He had actually been released!

Karol's experiences in the concentration camp were horrible and my father learned on that day, what was done to the people there, though of course he was not allowed to look behind the scenes. Karol's collection took place at the entrance to the camp, who would go in there voluntarily? Karol ate a whole loaf of bread in one go that night, and while doing so he described the daily routine in the camp.

It was Easter Sunday morning 1943 and everyone was still asleep when I was awakened by a noise that I could not figure out. The master bedroom door was open as usual and I heard whispers, Polish words with 'Hallelujah' in them. A delegation of our workers, mostly women, were standing with a bowl of water and a book in the master bedroom and sprinkled the water with a few twigs onto the now awakening parents.

Later that day, this old Polish custom expanded to a true water battle and over the next hour no one could walk across the courtyard staying dry. There were the men with a hose from the stable splashing and before they knew it some other workers fought back, armed with hoses from the factory. We watched them from the windows on the upper level of our house and we were in stitches. It was better than in the movies! The relationship with our workers was relaxed and no one took it the wrong way when someone penetrated into the bedrooms. The maids had probably opened the front door and let them in. The living conditions of the workers were rather tight, despite that they worked well and willingly. How bad it must have been for them in Poland, since they all tried to bring their relatives to us. These were of course not only able-bodied people, but also parents and grandparents. They had to obtain a special permit from an office and Dad had to sign it. The purchase of the bankrupt Staude estate was just right and the stables were converted into apartments, so as to create additional space next to the house. The spot, where the barn had been burned down by the former owner became a construction site for two large workers' homes, although they did not get finished at the end of the war. The employees told Dad that the old people in Poland would be deported. He then wrote a formal letter to the officials and asked them to consider the workload of his tannery and that the elderly would look after the grandchildren since both parents worked. The Kopalinski and Rospendek families both had four and five children under six years old. The garden between the old workers' house and the house of Ida Ernst was established as a playground and provided with a lawn. In addition, there was a pile of sand, swings and a seesaw. A bench for the babushkas (grandmothers) had also been set up and always put to good use.

A clever Polish shoemaker made good money with the production of summer shoes and repairs in addition to his wages.

I also had a pair and Mrs. Just had a pair made for Gisel for which she paid with produce. The shoes had soles made from old bicycle tires. Our people also had business with some shops in Heidau, for example, they made liquor from grain and potatoes, but this was officially strictly forbidden. One day the twenty-five-year-old fiancé of Lottka Ottolinska, I think his name was Stephan, was brought to the hospital. He had an alcohol poisoning and could not be saved. Shortly after, he was buried at the little Heidau cemetery right next to the church. The cause was probably only known to our parents, I knew about it later. Some Polish fellows had put together a small distillery and maybe their knowledge about the whole thing was not sufficient. Another Polish woman named Larissa was an art painter who worked in the factory. She showed me how to draw a rose and Olga cooked a traditional wheat meal in the communal kitchen which she shared with me sometimes. With these examples one can see that we all got along well.

When I was nine years of age a BDM leader (League of German Girls) asked me if I would like to be a leader - candidate and if I wanted to participate in the training every Sunday morning. Usually one got this call at the age of ten and so I rode my bicycle every Sunday morning to the town of Heinersdorf where many other girls unknown to me did the same training. We could not escape these calls and it was considered un-German to refuse. My parents knew this and so I finally had to give in. The details I cannot remember, but we sang the familiar songs and we learned all about the organization of the Hitler Youth on a blackboard. The attendance of these meetings was precisely documented. Ruth was ill one Sunday and could not attend the training. The following week she presented an apology written with a typewriter and she was asked who had signed it. They did not believe her that it was Mum's signature, accusing Ruth of forgery. Then it was checked with my parents and only when Mum's signature was acknowledged, they left her alone. Our parents were under suspicion anyway, because they were outsiders, and especially my father was being watched closely, for he never took part in political meetings. He always said there was a lot of work to be done and as the owner of a vital war supporting plant no one could harm him. So he beat them with their own means, but it was always a risk. Spies and traitors were scattered everywhere and we had to protect ourselves as much as possible. That was the main reason why he did not train with the horses. Mum had to show at the women's organization, but because of her profession she never took part at the meetings, which was equally brave and dangerous. With such actions you don't always make friends.

The great-grandmother on my mother's side must have been a heartless woman; she carried a closely guarded family secret. She was accused of mistreating an orphan child who had been included in the family and went to prison. She had not only beaten the underage girl but also had given her too little to eat, which was really hard because the girl had to work. Her husband alarmed the police and it is not known how long she was arrested. This wicked woman did not even give enough food to her own grandson Karl, Sigrid's father. Mum said that Uncle Karl had been a weak child.

The couple broke up the marriage, the great-grandfather lived in his parents' house with his brother (across from Löffel's) after the return of his former wife and Muttel took care of him. Anyway, the small farms in Klein-Bischwitz probably all had a so-called granny flat where the old people lived when their son or daughter took over the farm. Mum once told me that her grandmother had a piece of cultivated gardens and Karl took lilacs to the market in Breslau. There were six to eight lilac bushes, which she had stipulated for herself. Mum's father drove the milk every morning from the village with a horse-drawn carriage to the market and on the return trip he brought goods and medicine from Breslau, all the things the small farmers needed. He sold the milk to solid customers from the suppliers and he got a few percent for transport and sale for it. He often brought something for his children, but this changed dramatically when the First World War broke out in 1914 and he was drafted. Aunt Trude was the eldest of eight children and at the age of thirteen, after only seven years of school, she was needed at home and quit formal education. At first she had a farm hand, later a maid instead. Trude organized house and farm at such a young age including the horses and supplies. Uncle Ferdinand was born in 1911 as the youngest brother.

-6-

The Gestapo-Men in our House

Our factory signal horn replaced the clock for the surrounding farms - lunch was from 12.15 until one o'clock. Later, it was in action as an air raid siren when Dad was notified by telephone, but Heidau was never in real danger. There were two major attacks on Breslau, but luckily they did not result in big damages. They were Russian combat aircraft and in contrast to the Allied airmen they did not shoot very accurately.

Once a week Dad went to Liegnitz to buy food and clothes for the Ukrainian workers. The wages they earned as forced labourers had to be paid to the German government. The Ukrainians lived in barracks on the factory site, which were specially built for them.

Easter 1944 came and it meant separation from Gisel. She was allowed to go to the high school in Liegnitz and I was not. Dad would not let me because of the bomb threats in the city. I cried a lot for a few days and then had to resign myself to being taught in the next term in Heidau. Somehow I sensed that my dream of becoming a teacher burst right there and then. It was also the time when my understanding of the war changed. From then on, we all had to adjust a little bit more every day to the ever-changing situation - the time of playing was over for me. Horrible news arrived; the village was divided into supporters and opponents of the war. The opponents were in the majority, but could not violate new and existing laws. Politics were never discussed in public and the trust within the community was disturbed. We knew of brothers, who due to conflicting opinions and perceptions did not talk to each other anymore and became enemies.

After Easter, Gisel travelled daily by bus to the school in Liegnitz. She and some children from other villages were in a preparatory class to bring their knowledge to the level of the city children. In winter, she stayed with Just's friends in the city during the week and returned to Heidau on Fridays until the Christmas holidays.

On July 19th, 1944 we came home on the road from Parchwitz where we had bought gladioli for Dad's birthday. Wally told me that in a city in the Czech Republic they used to have a coal business. One day her father was picked up by the Nazis and taken to the concentration camp Theresienstadt because he was a Jew. Wladislava Pollock was Catholic but the two daughters were half-Jews, though, I believe, also Catholic. Once when I was sick in bed, Nelly came dressed as Santa Claus and brought self-baked cookies to me. It was very unusual for me that she came into my room in a bishop's suit with a purple cross and miter. The costume was made mostly of brown paper. She had made a long beard, but I recognized her in spite of it. Unusual for me because the Santa Claus we had in Silesia wore a red coat and a red hat with white fur trim. Back in Glockschütz, my first home, Dad had always played Santa Claus for us. When I was still very young we went shopping in Hundsfeld at one of the first winter days. Curiously, I had spotted a Santa Claus mask in a bag, but when Dad wore it later, I did not recognize him. In addition, he disguised his voice and even his pronunciation, and I was so fascinated by the whole scene that I could not imagine that it would be Dad or someone else in the family. Ruth later explained everything to me but I did not believe her.

One late afternoon in the first week of August my father got a surprise visit from two men of the **Ge**heime **Sta**ats**po**lizei (Gestapo=Secret State Police). They were dressed in dark leather coats and hats. Dad was informed by telephone and crossed the yard to our house. Together they went into Dad's office and after a short conversation they wanted to take him to Liegnitz. Dad got up from his chair and said it was not possible that evening because he had to clarify a few things in the factory and could not leave his men alone. He would contact the policemen the next morning. The two men then wanted to use our phone and call their superiors. Our phone had several additional buttons and one had to press a silver button to get a long distance line. Dad did not tell them how to use the phone and walked back to the factory. The men said to Mum, 'Show us how the phone works.'

Mum responded without hesitation, 'My husband did not show you, neither will I!'

The Gestapo-men then pressed all the buttons and eventually worked it out. They were unable to get a line because it was already after business hours and the telephone office was closed. The office was needed to make long distance calls. After a while they gave up and went into the yard and talked to one another. They did not go to the factory buildings since they were obviously too scared of the numerous workers. Both of them returned to the house and searched it top to bottom instead while Mum and we children were watching them.

Without any success they left the property soon after. Dad sent two Poles over to find out if it was safe to come back. All the time he had hidden under bundles of furs in the barn. Finally he appeared and we had dinner together, while Pauline shut the gate as usual. After breakfast the next morning Dad rang an office in Berlin. He explained the situation and asked them to rectify his problem. He said the production would stop immediately without him. At that time I was already on my way to school. Dad then took the DKW car and drove to Liegnitz where he was imprisoned for fourteen days and repeatedly interrogated. The officers read passages of an anonymous letter to him in which he was being accused of conspiracy. The letter said he would treat the foreign workers too well. He let them sing and make music in their quarters and supplied them with clothing and two prams. All this was against regulations. On top of things the workers were allowed to keep rabbits to improve their nutrition. Apparently the writer did not know about the goat milk which was mixed with cow's milk.

Dad also heard shots at the prison at night. It was the aftermath of the attempted assassination of Hitler which had taken place on July 20th. Dad was finally released with the help of his clients in Berlin and Breslau. Mum took over the reins in his absence and continued with the production at a lower rate. Later she received the Federal Cross of Merit for it.

In September, Dad met with the local head of the Farmers' Association, Mr. Köhler, in Heidau and talked about the incident. Mr. Köhler said he would try to get the letter in question. He succeeded in mid-December and Dad saw a disguised handwriting that was somehow familiar to him. He covered various spots when he showed the letter to his mother Pauline. She said without hesitation that it was the handwriting of her husband Hans Krause. Pauline and my parents never mentioned it to anyone. They had to be very careful not to attract attention. Dad was already known to the Gestapo and did not want to be questioned again. Krause was dangerous and as I recall, Pauline never really loved him.

Our father was not only an entrepreneur and family man, but he also held an unexpected honorary position. He was asked by two Ukrainians and their fiancées to marry them. My father asked the mayor and learned that foreigners were not allowed to be married officially and therefore not even our pastor could help. Of course, all participants knew that Dad had no official powers, but at this time, on that day, no one cared. Dad agreed and there was a little, pitiful ceremony. We did not know how long the war would last and so they got married only with their hearts and mutual promises. Dad also typed up two documents, signed them and put the company's stamp underneath.

We had about twenty to twenty-five Ukrainians in the company who were forced labourers. The rest were Poles and Czechs, who did not find work in their home countries. Our daily production amounted to five thousand rabbit skins.

Once a week, there was a bath day for the workers in the wet area of the factory. It was all scheduled and we never had a problem there. Gisel and I caught up again on her birthday on January 12th, 1945. The Christmas holidays marked the end of our school time in Silesia. After the holidays, there was one last traditional game hunt and shortly afterwards the first convoy of refugees came from the east through our village. On January 28th, 1945 Heidau was evacuated after thousands of refugees had already taken the long walk from Breslau to Berlin through the village. It was devilishly cold, every night minus 30 degrees Celsius (-22 Fahrenheit) and we were fortunate to have enough heating supplies for the winter. We had a bricked-up room in the basement, where supposedly a full wagon load of coal was kept. In January our stocks of all essential things were still very good. Because of the factory we had some advantages, e.g. we were able to store salt and sacks of wheat and potatoes.

As Heidau was being evacuated Aunt Frieda came to us. She rode her bicycle fifty kilometers through snow and ice, since the roads were clogged and the inhabitants of Klein-Bischwitz were diverted to the Czech Republic. There was no more space on Dad's truck for her and so she decided to take the bike. She arrived exhausted at our place and for a little woman as she was, it was a tremendous achievement. Dad brought Muttel with five small children and luggage by truck from Klein-Bischwitz. There were Ruth Löffel, Aunt Frieda's daughter, born in 1941, Manfred, 1941, Paul 1940 and the two children of Uncle Ferdinand, Peter and Irmgard, who were just as old, none of them went to school yet. The other mothers and Aunt Trude should meet with us later. Three teams consisting of Aunt Frieda, Emma, Muttel and the children travelled towards Saxony.

Sleeping bags of rabbit furs were quickly made for the five children. Our three lambskin sleeping bags were made by Wally in our kitchen. It was too cold in the factory during the day. Dad turned the heater on in the evenings for the refugees who parked their carriages in the yard and stayed at the factory for the night. Our chimney heralded heat from afar, and later it served as a reference point for the Russian troops.

German troops came from Norway to Silesia in order to fight back the Soviets. A company of about two hundred and fifty soldiers set up camp for a fortnight on one of our fields. Wally made gloves out of rabbit fur for the officers in exchange for coffee. Then one night the camp was removed and we did not know where they had gone, but there were only two possibilities: they either went east, to stop the Soviets at the Oder River, or they headed west to defend Liegnitz. The troops all looked so similar, rough and unshaven. Some were very skinny and I was wondering where they should find the strength to fight. Miss Mantell, our teacher, was cooking for the refugees in the kitchen at school. I was there countless hours peeling potatoes. Every day we made boiled potatoes with onion sauce and sauerkraut. Anything else was no longer available.

Dad gave Kasimir as coachman to our relatives. He was a captured French soldier, who was glad to get away and my parents trusted him to be reliable. Once a month he received a parcel from France and when there was a block of chocolate in it, he would share it with us. He justified the trust, as Aunt Frieda reported later. He took care of the people entrusted to him and only went in the direction of France after he had placed his charges in Zeicha, Saxony. Kasimir had worked several years for us. He was boarded with us and had his meals in the kitchen, but at a different table. The distance had to be maintained for political reasons and we never knew when an inspection would be performed. Being too close to foreigners was punishable. The Polish girls were employed at the household and sat at our table, for they were regular employees. Our front door was always unlocked then. One had to expect German officials to come in on Sundays and stick their beaks into the pots. The Heidau SA-men

(Storm Detachment) were well organized, but they trusted us to a certain point or they had relevant commands. I know that our neighbours were searched several times, but I cannot remember a thorough search in our house. They came every Sunday and very boldly picked up our horses and took them for a fun ride.

Dad never rode with them, instead, he was very angry because the horses had to work in the fields and truly deserved a day's rest. There were some good horses, slender and beautiful, I loved them all, and later I missed them a lot, for I grew up with them and considered them my friends who had to be treated with respect. Seeing other men on our horses did hurt me a lot. I was powerless, I felt ignored and betrayed. The SA-men were farmers from Heidau and they only had workhorses not suitable for riding. Tractors were rare and all the farmers relied on their horses. So these guys came to us and then spent hours with our animals. We watched them helplessly as they rode off....

The Lilie family from Breslau, customers of Dad's, consisted of the parents, their daughter and daughter-in-law, Mrs. Brand with a little son. They came in the days after the evacuation of the village and stayed in the dining room and music room. There was also an elderly lady, Mrs. Kanus. The company in Breslau was called 'Kanus and Lilie.' Dad drove them to the train station in Liegnitz, but there were no longer trains in operation and so they all had to come back to Heidau.

At the same time Dad had two truck loads of finished rabbit furs ready to go to the Air Force but had no fuel coupons left for the transport. He was waiting for a call to pick them up from Liegnitz but the call never came. Today I think he did not want to leave Heidau anyway, and the wait for the coupons was only a pretext for the police, who told everyone to leave immediately. Why else did he have fake Polish ID's for himself, Mum and Ruth in his possession? The truck was not loaded, nothing was actually prepared. I did not have any thoughts at this time that our family would remain in Heidau all alone. Uncle Otto came with his wife Klara and their young son Erhard by van to our place. It was on the last day of evacuation and he begged Dad to join them, but Dad rejected. After a short stay we said goodbye and they drove further west to Liegnitz, where they came under fire. They had to seek cover in a ditch and German soldiers almost pinched their car in the process. With difficulty Otto was able to defend his vehicle and managed to escape.

-7-

February 8th and a difficult Decision

It was the morning of February 8th, 1945 when I was awakened at about six thirty by the loud thunder of one or more guns. This was new for us children and we ran into the master bedroom. Dad was already up standing at the window. We ran over to him and also tried to see something, but it was still too dark. Dad firmly said, 'Get dressed quickly, hurry!' Ruth and I obeyed without question. Mum got up too and took care of Ursula. A few minutes later, Ruth and I were ready; we had combed our hair in a rush and quickly went back to our father. The artillery fire had died down and there was an eerie silence all around. It was the calm before the storm. Dad, Ruth and I went up to one of the rooms under the roof and looked through the window.

'Our barn in Dahme is burning,' said Dad softly, almost toneless, and he knew he could not save it. It was full of un-threshed wheat and rye. Russian troops set fire to many buildings in order to drive people out. It was terrible and I felt an indescribable fear. We looked to the left and saw Russian tanks approaching from the direction of Parchwitz, rolling over the Schäferberg (a hill) to Heidau. I saw soldiers running into our yard and I did not know if they were Germans or Russians. Then all hell broke loose. The guns fired with a terrible noise and the whole house was shaking. Dad grabbed my hand and together we rushed down the stairs into the basement immediately. There we found many Poles and Ukrainians already gathered. There must have been a total of sixty; the various cellars were full of people. Grandma Pauline and Hans Krause had arrived too and waited on the left side near the wall. On the opposite side, we found Mum who was holding Ursula by the hand. In everyone's face I saw fear, only fear. My heart was beating up to my throat and I never wanted to let go of Daddy's hand ever again. The basement was freezing, but out of sheer fear I did not feel the cold. There we all stood in darkness and nobody said anything. At this moment, Grandma Pauline opened the basement door and went upstairs in the dark. We could not believe it. Krause told us that she had forgotten her handbag with her papers and she wanted to collect it from her apartment. Dad was angry because it was now too late to stop her. A minute later we heard a bullet hitting an upstairs window. Shortly thereafter we heard Pauline crying for help. Without hesitation, Dad ran upstairs and two Poles went with him. The rest of us waited with dismay. It did not take long for the men to return with Pauline. They carried her back into the basement badly injured, put her down on the extra bed and bandaged her temporarily. A bullet had hit her arm, she was bleeding but it was not life threatening. The strike had broken the window pane and splinters of glass were swirled through the room and unfortunately she was hit by several of them. For me it was an indescribable shock and I could not even do anything for her. Almost simultaneously, the basement door suddenly burst open and loud shouts in Russian ordered us to come upstairs. We only had been in the basement for about half an hour. A few Poles were the first to leave, because they were closest to the stairs. Without turning around, they went upstairs, nobody said a word. Dad was still holding me by the hand and after about fifteen more Poles had gone up it was our turn. I no longer felt my knees and clung to Dad. Together we went up, where we faced an entirely new situation: it was bright and scary.

In the front of the hallway there was our garden table and the soldiers were sitting on the respective chairs. They ordered us to show our ID's, while others with guns were ready to fire and looked at everyone who passed the cellar door. Dad presented his Polish passport and it was checked with disdain. When they saw me I looked down and my dad pulled me away. After we passed the first inspection the Poles were treated the same way. Mum came a little later with Ursula among Polish women, and after her Ruth with more Polish women.

After this first check, we all stood in the snowy courtyard, men and women separated. It was way below zero and we froze like never before. The horror did not end here. Machine guns were set up hastily and I got scared to death because I was afraid they would now shoot us all. Was this the end of my short life? All were silent, no one moved. I was still holding Daddy's hand as tight as I possibly could. Suddenly the guns were fired with a thunder and at first I did not know what was happening. I had my eyes closed, but was not hit. Then I opened them and saw what was going on. The bullets were not meant for us, but for the locks of the stables and barns. A quick sigh of relief from all of us. Some soldiers smashed the hunting rifles on the stones of the porch steps which they took from the locked gun cabinet in the office. The remaining horses were led out of the stable and three soldiers quickly mounted them. The stallion was not yet broken in, got up with his front legs and threatened to run. He was beaten on the head with a shovel by the Russians until he was seriously injured and dropped to the ground bleeding. Then they pulled him back up and dragged him away. Meanwhile, someone had brought Grandma Pauline back into her apartment. I detached myself from the group and sneaked up the stairs. The door was ajar and I could hear her heavy breathing. Grandma Pauline lay on the sofa in her living room and looked at me silently and helplessly. I held the door handle tightly in my hand and dared not go inside because we must not speak German, or belong to this house. She might have spoken in German, and thus give us away. I did not think it would be a farewell forever, although I had a horrible feeling in my stomach. As much as I wanted to go and help her it was impossible. I regretted that I was so young. Looking at her face was the saddest moment in my young life. Why is this all happening, I thought. I was confused and did not know what to do next. Eventually I turned around and slowly walked down the stairs. Each step I took reluctantly, perhaps I was still waiting for a lifeline and an inspiration. It did not come. With a heavy heart I went back outside. Meanwhile, it was afternoon and we were all relegated to a barn opposite the house, where we still had some bundles of fur we could sit on. From there, we saw how the soldiers went to work at our house wearing white aprons. The day before our men had slaughtered a pig which was now in the hands of the Soviets. None of us in the barn got any pork from them; we probably could not have eaten anything anyway. Later that night we were allowed to leave the barn, but could not go back to our house, which was occupied by the Russians. We had to find shelter for the night because the barn was too cold. The five of us went two doors down to a neighbouring house owned by the Alteheld family. Polish workers had already lived there for a few days since our neighbours had left and looked after the remaining cows and chickens. So at least they had milk and eggs, and they showed us to the bedroom upstairs. I remember two beds in a sparsely furnished room. It was all dark, and since we had no candles there was no light. We had to find our way in the dark. Anyway, we had two beds, warm blankets and even pillows. We only took off our shoes and covered up as best as we could. It took a while until we were warm and fell asleep. Since that night, we always slept in our clothes in fear of attacks. We neither had food nor water for over twenty-four hours. This day changed our lives forever; nothing was like it used to be. What would be waiting for us tomorrow? How much worse could it get?

On this snowy day, a tragedy occurred in the Jüttner family. During the Russian invasion, a massacre took place in Heidau. The Polish servant of the farmer Mr. Jüttner told a soldier, he had been badly treated. Whether this was true or not, I can't say. Subsequently, the whole family was killed and with them thirty German refugees who had been caught by the Russians. Days later, the old neighbour Mrs. Grindel dared to go to the abandoned farm and found the bodies in the barn. Liesel Jüttner was seriously injured and lay among the dead family members. She was found more dead than alive. On the same day in February several old men I did not know were killed, and Gerda Dittrich said they were strangers.

It was a relatively quiet night - Heidau had surrendered without a fight. The battle front seemed to have moved further to the west. The next morning we went without breakfast back into our yard. It was eerie and quiet. I was very cold and I took Dad's hand again. We looked around; there were no Russians to see. They had left Heidau very early that morning. What should we do now? There were about twenty of our Polish workers in the yard and Dad went right over to talk to them. I joined Mum and my sisters and together we went into our house. It was obvious that some of the soldiers had stayed there. Dad came in and told us to pack our things. The Pollock family came downstairs and gave us a hand. Mum put sheets and blankets into new Hessian bags. The dishes and china were packed into large brown baskets with two handles. We, the children, were in the hallway outside the kitchen and helped as best as we could. Wagons were prepared by the men outside to leave. Dad did not need to tell them to hurry. They had so much fear that they trusted him blindly. They all wanted to get away. It was unanimously decided to go to Poland, in order to avoid more Russians. Dad gave me the order to fetch Ruth's Communion candle from the attic and I hurried off. We wanted to take it with us for it was quite long. In my absence, another Russian unit with trucks came to our snow covered yard. Soldiers jumped off and threatened all with their guns, and everything came to a halt. They yelled, ' Uri, Uri,' (the German word is Uhr) and pushed the adults around. By this they meant 'Bring on the watches!' Watches were precious and easy to carry. Dad had no watch any more, even the beautiful pocket watch, which he had usually carried in his breast pocket of his jacket on work days, no longer existed. Both had already been taken from him the day before. Now the Russians were angry and indignant, and shoved Dad away from the group into the horse stables. He was probably chosen because he was better dressed than the other men and therefore was considered a leader. As soon as I returned with the candle, a soldier grabbed it from me. What a shock and a disappointment! I promised myself to be more careful in the future and hide treasures of this kind in my clothes.

Our father was as white as a sheet when he came out of the stables, followed by the three soldiers who threatened him with guns. What exactly they had done to him out of sight we can only guess. He never talked about it, perhaps not even with Mum. Dad walked up to Mum who had just thrown a bag of clothes on our wagon. She should get her jewellery box from its hiding place and give it to the soldiers. Then in great haste she emptied another bag and the jewelry fell into the snow. Her gold watch was no longer there because it too had been taken from her by the very first group of Russians. Now the Russians were not satisfied with the contents of the box in which also Ruth's Communion jewellery was kept. They screamed at first and then took it all. Again, we all were threatened with guns and yelled at. We stood there and did not move. We had nothing more to give and I think Dad showed his empty pockets. After a short while I went back into the house. In that military unit were some men who obviously knew no water closets, for they drank from the bowl. I did not understand that. Others were fighting over a bottle of perfume which they also drank because it contained alcohol. Later we found one of our typewriters in the ditch after the Soviets had learned that it did not make any music. It became clear that they had never seen such a machine. Somehow the situation relaxed for the better, perhaps because they had to move on. Anyway, the oxen were now attached and we left the yard with four covered wagons on the paved road towards Parchwitz. The Pollock-women did not come with us but instead tried their luck walking on foot towards Czechoslovakia. We never saw them again and I hope to this day that they survived. The Poles had loaded their belongings on wagons and walked alongside. Mum, Ursula and I sat on a wagon with tires on which the possessions of the Michner family was also to be found. Dad and Ruth went on foot, while Ruth still pushed her beautiful bike. However, it was taken from her by a Russian after about two kilometers. With heavy hearts we left Grandma Pauline and Hans Krause behind. Dad had gone upstairs for the last time to check on his injured mother. She was not fit for travel and he had to protect his family. It must have been a hopeless challenge for my desperate father to make that decision. A dramatic situation, no doubt.

With indescribable fury and resignation we started our journey. On a hill called 'Schäferberg' Dad sent Ruth up to us onto the wagon, because there were many bodies of German soldiers in the snow, covered in blood. They were spread all over the place, most of them had no coats anymore and their bare feet could be seen from the distance. It was a scene of horror; the snow was red with blood. This was a sight I will never forget in my whole life. All along the route dead German soldiers were lying in the trenches. I only saw the right side of the road because the hood of my new sheepskin sleeping bag blocked the view to the left side. But I'm sure it looked exactly the same over there. We three children had the sheepskin bags with enclosed slots for our hands and we were not freezing yet. The whole group was supposed to move east, but had to make a big circle around the disputed territory of Breslau, and so we went north towards the Oder River. It is the same hill of Schäferberg, where Frederick the Great had given the famous speech to his officers, on the eve of the Battle of Leuthen after it became known that the enemy approached with overwhelming numbers.

The battle took place on December 5th, 1757 during the Seven Years' War. The Prussian King Frederick II fought against the Austrian army under the leadership of Prince Karl Alexander of Lorraine. Frederick's campaign plan was to quickly beat the main enemy Austria in Bohemia, before France and Russia could come to their aid.

'Gentlemen, as you know, the Duke of Lorraine succeeded in conquering Schweidnitz (Swidnica), to beat the Duke of Severn and take possession of Breslau, while I was forced to bring the progress of the French and imperial nations to halt. A part of Silesia and the province's capital Breslau with all the supplies for the war were lost thereby. In fact, my embarrassments would be at the insuperable pitch, had I not boundless trust in you, and your qualities, which have been so often manifested, as soldiers and sons of your country. Hardly anyone among you has not distinguished himself by some nobly memorable action: all these services to the State and me I know well, and will never forget and I flatter myself, therefore, you will also not be lacking now in what the State is entitled to demand of your bravery. The hour is at hand. I should think I had done nothing, if I left the Austrians in possession of Silesia. I intend, in spite of the Rules of Art, to attack Prince Karl's Army, which is nearly thrice our strength, wherever I find it. The question is not of his numbers, or the strength of his chosen position. I have to take that step, or all is lost! We need to beat the enemy or let us bury all before his batteries. Please, make this my decision announced to all officers and soldiers of the Army; prepare the men for what work is now to ensue, and say that I hold myself entitled to demand exact fulfillment of orders.

When I reflect that you are Prussians, can I think that you will act unworthily? But if there should be the one or the other who dreads to share all dangers with me, he,'--continued his Majesty, with an interrogative look, and then pausing to answer, --'can have his discharge this evening, and shall not suffer the least reproach from me.'--Modest strong bass murmur; meaning 'No, by the Eternal!'

At this point, the Major Konstantin von Billerbeck interrupted: 'That would be an infamous scoundrel indeed!' Frederick ended his speech: 'Even beforehand, I was certain you would not leave. So I count on your help and for the victory. If I fall and do not reward you for your services, then your country will have to do it. Now go back to the camp and repeat to the regiments, what you have heard from me. One more thing, gentlemen: the cavalry regiment that does not relentlessly crash into the enemy when it is ordered will be turned into a garrison regiment after the battle. Now farewell, my lords! In a short time we will have beaten the enemy, or we will never see each other again.' The battle was won. And so there we were, 188 years later, with our own enemies and battles to face....

Our journey continued. At a slow pace we travelled through the snow and I had the impression that we were the only people left in the country. I was scared. Mum was scared too and I always kept close to her, it was just natural. Silently, the hours went by and the way seemed endless. My stomach was empty and the first cramps occurred. After a few kilometers we saw a group of Russian soldiers who came toward us. They looked at us disapprovingly, but left us alone. Again and again we saw Russian troops on their way to Berlin.

In the evening we stopped at a village because of the severe cold and there we found a guest house with a hall attached to the main building. The floor was covered with straw and we ended up spending the night there. Suddenly out of nowhere Russian soldiers showed up and did a head count of the group. We were trapped again! We children got back into our sleeping bags that we had taken off for the short walk from the wagon to the hall. All the others had blankets, clothes and whatever cover they could use for warmth. However, before we got to sleep the hall door was kicked open with force, and the soldiers lit up the faces of the prisoners with burning pieces of wood. They pointed at the women who should come along with them. Dad tucked Ruth's head under the blanket and so she was not discovered, therefore not counted. The Russians knew the total number and as it turned out that a woman was missing, it got loud. Dad asked Mrs. Swoboda, who was not chosen because of her advanced age, to go instead of Ruth. Everyone knew that the selected women were to be raped. She had no children and her husband was a soldier. She nodded without hesitation, got up and went bravely to her fate. I gave her a memorial in my heart; I will not forget this brave sacrifice.

Ruth's friend from her time in Glockschütz named Rosel Priwattke had hanged herself in an attic after the first night the Soviets came to her place. She could not live with the memory of a Russian rape. This, of course, we learned much later and there were many more suicides. The communist leader Stalin encouraged his troops to rape German girls and women. The next day we got up and without breakfast made our way to the town of Steinau on the Oder River. We only had a few bites of bread while sitting on the wagon. As we came closer to the bridge we were stopped by Russian troops because the bridge had been severely damaged in combat and was no longer usable. The Russians ordered all the Polish men to repair it. Dad was officially a Pole now, and thus was also affected. The rest of us were looking for a house close by and the women made fires in the stoves. We found a ladder leading to the attic and immediately a small group of young men and women decided to hide up there from the Russians. Ruth climbed up with them, then the attic ladder was pulled up and the trap door was locked from the top. Ruth and the others were safe for now. Together with the Poles, we lived in this small abandoned house for a week and in its kitchen we cooked for all the residents. There was not much food and we were getting weaker, our faces changed quickly. We were half frozen, tired and always hungry. Our clothes suffered of course, we could only patch them up at best. The cover of our wagon was stolen in the first night. Even most of our belongings had disappeared after a short time. We now had no blankets and sleeping bags left. For me it was the next shock. What else could they possibly take from us? We had lost everything, we were hungry and I could not imagine what would happen tomorrow. All we had was our family. I ached all over and like the others, I was totally exhausted. Nobody talked about the future anymore or that we would live in peace again. I trusted my parents more than I can put into words today. Those were my thoughts in the cold and hopelessness. We children had been taught not to lie and now we had to constantly lie and play roles in order to survive. A single mistake or treachery of some sort would have destroyed our chances in an instant. I stayed right next to Ursula and Mum, who with the other women had to wash the clothes of the Russians. After pouring our waste water into the manure pile in front of the house the legs of a dead woman became visible. It was a terrible sight, but I do not think it surprised me. The Lilie family had come with us to Steinau, but on a different wagon. In Steinau somebody from the family asked me if I would take their four-year-old boy for a walk in the fresh air. None of them dared to go into the street and they thought the children were safe. I took him and told him not to speak so the soldiers would not realize that we were Germans. But as children are, he did not keep his mouth shut. I realized that the risk was simply too big and I had to make a quick decision. So I turned around and walked back into the house with him. There I was received with amazement and being asked why we were back again so soon. I was afraid, I said to the child's mother and someone from the family looked at me, and told the boy that he should say in German 'good day, sir,' if a soldier was around. At that moment I was lost for words. Can anyone be so naive? As if a Russian soldier armed with a machine gun would hold back. At that point in time we had not heard of the atrocities the Red Army committed against children. Countless infants and young children were thrown with full force against the walls until they were dead while their mothers were watching. The soldiers still made jokes about the lifeless, bleeding bodies when they left them behind. They smashed their skulls beyond recognition with hard kicks. After the babies were killed, the older siblings and mothers were raped and beaten in the cruelest way, in many cases to death. A lot of the surviving women then took their lives. I never took the boy for a walk again.

After a week of hard and arduous work, the men made the almost impossible possible: one lane of the bridge was repaired. Our father looked very tired and had minor injuries to his hands and knees. There was still too little food and the mood was getting even worse. Dad gave our wagon and one ox to a group of Poles, who then went over the repaired bridge to the east. The German family named Michner drove with them. In one of the stables Daddy found an old handcart with wooden wheels and attached the remaining ox to it. Dad did not give up and made a bold decision: he was fluent in Polish and declared to the Russians that he had to pick up his sick mother. He seemed credible and they let us go. We loaded our luggage onto the large handcart and started our journey back towards Heidau. En route we were stopped several times by soldiers and Dad had to tell his story again and again. Mum sat bent over and wrapped up on the wagon and had her headscarf pulled deep into her face. She played dumb and sick, which she did very convincingly. Her Polish language skills were not sufficient and Dad chose this tactic in order to fool any soldiers. Ruth was hidden under the luggage and had to keep absolutely still while Dad walked in front on the left of the ox and led it with a rope. Ursula and I walked freezing in the snow alongside the cart. We did not speak at all, we had nothing to say. It was far too exhausting in the cold. We still saw dead bodies on both sides of the road; they had even less clothes on than the first time we saw them. It was a gruesome sight and cannot be compared to anything I had ever seen before. I looked into their empty eyes and rigid faces contorted with pain. That picture haunted me for a long time in my dreams. This time we could no longer be protected by Dad. Our shoes were wet, we had cold feet and the track seemed just as endless as on the way to Steinau.

By late afternoon we arrived back home and our dachshund Strolch came running joyfully toward us. Dad's hunting dog had already been killed during the invasion. In the yard there were Russian soldiers and one of them took Strolch into an army truck. Thus the last of our pets was gone and I mourned. I wanted to cry, but there were no more tears. And it got worse.

-8-

Grandmother Pauline

Our injured grandmother had died on the eleventh of February. The old Krause had found a doctor who treated the wound, but it was in vain. A piece of glass from the broken window, which was destroyed by the Russian bullet, had found its way to her heart. When we got home our dear Grandma Pauline lay already buried in the garden. Krause had wrapped her body in unused rubber aprons from the tannery, and buried her without a coffin all by himself.

My disappointment and despair was immense; I could not imagine a future without her. We had reached a point where only the here and now counted. From now on it was a matter of surviving day to day. I think in those days I grew up to become an adult. I had no other choice, the days of fun and games were long gone, I could not even remember my last laugh anymore. I saw everything around me developing for the worse and I was insecure, which was new to me. The last days had been so cruel that I did not believe I could ever trust another adult again apart from the family members. I was very cold.

The ox was tired and Dad brought the poor animal into the goat barn. The goats had been stolen, and two days later the same happened to the ox. Our closets and wardrobes had been emptied, only a few pieces of clothing lay on the floor. We brought everything back in order as best as we could and it was clear that we hardly had anything left to wear. Dad was being sent to collect the cows that wandered in the woods. They roared with pain, for they had to be milked. He wore a white bandage around his arm and was fitted with identification documents. The cows were then cared for in the stables. The year before Dad had bought dyestuff for the tannery and stored the containers in the attic for a new beginning after the war because he feared that prices would rise dramatically. The Russians had left such disarray that the powder was mixed with sugar syrup and everything was now completely useless. He had also ordered a modern Claas thresher, paid 20,000 Reichsmarks for it, but it was never delivered because of the war. We never got our money back either.

Russian trucks drove off with our supplies; Mum and I carried coals, briquettes and wheat in buckets into our basement and into the oven in the hallway. We were left alone and no one sent us away. The holdings were so large that we had enough time to save what could be saved. At first we slept in Grandma Pauline's kitchen because it was warm there, since we could not heat the other rooms anymore. The beds were positioned near the kitchen window, so that the basin was blocked. There was no more water anyway. In addition, there was no electricity, no radio, no telephone and no newspaper. We found ourselves back in the Stone Age; the period of harsh limitations began. The shops were closed and what you did not have now was very difficult, if not impossible to get. There was for example no more detergent; we found a container with a wool detergent for mink in the tannery, which we used for ourselves, clothes and dishes.

The Dittrich family had already fled on January 21st, 1945 with a wagon, two horses and two oxen toward the town of Zeicha, Saxony, which was about 270 kilometers away. They were accompanied by their relatives, the Tschäpe and Menzel families who also had their wagons and animals. They did not get very far because an axle broke on Dittrich's wagon in Kunitz. They fled without the wagon and made it to Fellendorf on the ninth of February. They were taken off guard by Russian troops, who used their Stalin-organs (a nickname for a Russian weapon) that were widely heard. The Russians sent the three families and the Fellendorf population with a single evacuation back to the east. They reached Gross-Beckern near Liegnitz on the first day. On the second day, they arrived in Kunitz and stayed a fortnight with a cousin of the Menzel family. Mrs. Dittrich and Mrs. Menzel, both about sixty, went on foot to Heidau to see whether the house was still standing and if they could live there. There was only one man in the group, Mr. Ernst Dittrich, who was over seventy years of age. Shortly after all three families came back to Heidau. The people of Fellendorf remained in Kunitz until the Russian front continued to move west. We did not receive a message what ever happened to them. We met the three families weeks later, since nobody dared to leave their houses for some time and so no one knew of the presence of the others.

-9-

Our Father Artur

On March 1st, 1945 three Russians appeared in long black leather coats in our yard. Mum had just baked a cake without eggs for my eleventh birthday. Eggs were in extremely short supply, but Mum somehow managed to do without them. The heavenly smell of the cake was in the air and I could not wait to eat a piece when those three men were asking Dad for directions. Ruth accompanied him and saw him getting in a car with them and together they left the yard in the direction of Liegnitz. I stood at the window and was quite confused. Dad would not go away on my special day, would he?

He did not return that day and Mum and Ruth tried to comfort me. The next day we waited hopefully for his return, for it was not the first time that he had been taken from our property. Perhaps it was one of the frequent interrogations and then they would let him off again, we thought. There was no news on the second day and then we were not sure if we would ever see him again. No one knew of Krause's wickedness, from which we suffered. The worst part was that he had slandered Dad and we thought that must have been why he did not come back.

One day in April Ruth was just using Neumann's outhouse, when she heard engine noises in the courtyard and looked with horror through the small heart-shaped opening in the door. Two Russian military trucks stopped and the engines were cut. Twenty soldiers jumped off and two of them broke the entrance door to Neumann's home. They went in and found a young girl alone with a broken leg in the living room. Mrs. Neumann was away and so the soldiers had an easy victim. The poor girl was raped by all twenty of them, mercilessly. Ruth did not know that there was a girl, because it was only the day before when she lodged with Mrs. Neumann. Her mother was looking for a place to stay and also for a cart for her daughter. The two of them were all on their own since her father had been killed in the war. Ruth had to be absolutely quiet in the outhouse and she was understandably scared. She did not want to attract one or several soldiers by making a noise. It took a long time until the soldiers finished their dirty game. They came out drunk. They had brought a few bottles of vodka with them since there was no more alcohol in any of the houses. Fate had spared Ruth once more and when she felt safe, she came home and told us with a tremor, what she had seen. Mrs. Neumann later talked to Mum and we only then learned of the terrible experience of the girl. The old woman blamed herself that she had left the house, but what could she have done against armed men? There was no morality, no justice. Every day was a struggle for survival and often I was afraid of losing my family. Due to the meager food we were all weak and I remember that I had pretty much forgotten the taste of fresh fruit and chocolate. We lived in our house, but we had lost our home. The people around us had changed; the street scene reflected back the whole catastrophe. Where we used to play the ground was soaked with blood and sometimes we found ammunition parts and uniform buttons. We never picked them up and always walked around them. Maybe it was punishable to be caught with these items and we therefore did not want to take chances. One of my classmates was raped and abused very badly by Russian soldiers on the road to Liegnitz. I never saw her again, because she and her mother left Heidau shortly thereafter without leaving a message. Her father was killed in the final days of the war in Berlin and it was rare to receive any news, because in the general chaos almost everything was lost. We lived in total isolation, messages were transmitted only verbally. Sometimes German refugees from the western areas came to us on the way to their old homes when they saw smoke rising from our chimney. Then they asked for some food and camped for the night. We took in as many as we could and listened to their stories. In every family there were dead and missing persons, there were no more prospects for improvement for us. I thought we would have to flee and hide forever, and we would never have money and decent meals again.

-10-

Ruth's Hiding Spot and the Journey with Hilda

Hans Krause was in charge of the payroll since the time in Glockschütz, which turned out to be a bad decision. Shortly before the end of the war our tax advisor Mr. Schieweg went through the books and found out that Krause had embezzled the company. He funded his annual holidays with his daughter Greta in Königsberg in Upper Silesia with parts of the wages. Back then all the money was paid in cash weekly, none of the workers had a bank account. Each week we received a payment from the Eichborn Bank in the mail. Mum had a bunch of keys on her belt and had access to the vault. Compared to Hans Krause's later crimes, embezzlement of money was only a trifle.

Dad was being held in Liegnitz. Mr. Seidel, owner of the clubhouse in Parchwitz, was dismissed because of his age and dropped by in early May 1945 on his way home to tell us all about what had happened to Dad. Dad had been taken to prison by the Russians because of his age of forty years. Only men of seventy and over were sent home after questioning. The prisoners camped in the open air in an enclosed and guarded area. Krause was suddenly picked up by the Soviets and brought to Liegnitz for interrogation. During the hearings after the Russian invasion he described our father as a Nazi and later he said to Mum, 'Artur will not come back, I made sure of that!' He thought Mum would now get involved with him.

Before Krause returned, Mrs. Neumann stayed at our place. We spread out mattresses on the bedroom floor. Mrs. Neumann was sleeping in the same room; she and Mum still had beds. At that point we lived in my grandma's apartment, because the Ukrainian women occupied our living room downstairs. They not only looked after our cows but also after the animals of the neighbours. Mum and Ruth had to give them a hand and got milk for their work. Ruth could not milk until then, but she picked it up quickly. The old Krause slept on the living room sofa on which my dear grandmother had died.

Mrs. Neumann lost her disabled son during the Russian invasion. Two deserted German soldiers were hiding in her barn, but they were found and all three of them were shot dead within seconds. She buried the three bodies in her garden behind the house. Similarly, on the same day two old men who lived with their wives in small workers' cottages on the main street, lay sick in their beds and were unable to flee. All of them were killed.

I do not know whether Mrs. Neumann's husband was also killed or had died shortly before. In any case, Mrs. Neumann became a rather confused woman who announced every morning that she would sleep at home the next night because the shutters rattled at our house so she could not sleep. The stress and anxiety took their toll. For months, every other night we had Russian supply troops in the courtyard and officers in the house. Our luck was that the Ukrainians, who inhabited the ground floor, provided them with the essentials. At that time hardly any soldier came upstairs to our quarters. The women made themselves blouses out of the kitchen curtains.

In case we would be confronted by Russians Dad had instructed us as follows: Ruth had to faint, Mum would catch her, Ursula should be screaming and go for a pee on the bucket, and I should get some water. As it happened, we did just that and hoped for the best. Our faces were always as white as chalk. We were lucky.

I hate to imagine what Dad must have suffered knowing he was leaving us alone in this hell. Mum and we kids were totally unprepared, almost helpless. But we developed survival strategies that he had not thought existed. He had the well for drinking water uncovered shortly before his pickup. We would have had big problems with that heavy stone. He showed us how to draw the water and told us to keep a little fire burning in the stove, in case we should run out of matches. He showed this to all of us, but how was he to know that we would do it, too? Sometimes the fire went out in the summer months and so I went to the neighbours' maid with kindling and lit it back up. It was the very same neighbour who helped us to secure the front doors. The front door opened to the inside and so he put up heavy iron hooks on the right and left side of the door and placed a solid iron bar across. The heavy oak door was secure for now, but often we had to open it when the soldiers threatened to burn down the house. The rear door to the garden opened to the outside and so a wooden beam was tied around the doorknob with a rope and turned until it was stuck firmly against the door frame. During the days the doors were locked with keys only, because Ruth had to be able to flee when threatened through the opposite door. Of course there were also times when Russian soldiers stood at the front and the back at the same time. Ruth then immediately ran to the basement, which also had an exit to the garden. This basement was equipped as an air raid shelter and no one else went there. After Dad was in captivity, Mum got very ill and Ruth had to be hidden. The old Krause showed his true colours then. I developed a sense of responsibility at a rate that in retrospect now seems unlikely even to me. But it did happen that way, and I was nicknamed "Mummy" for it.

Around this time, Dad's brother Otto fell into U.S. captivity on German soil. He and his family had finally made it to West Germany. Now he had to go hungry and had no contact with them. The hunger was so bad that some of the prisoners even ate grass. After about half a year he was set free.

A Russian officer came into our room and greeted us in German with 'Good day.' Ruth was hiding while Ursula and myself were standing behind Mum for protection, and did not move. The officer spoke a little German, and began to talk with Mum. Maybe he wanted to test his language skills. He sounded like he did understand the language even before the war. At that moment I heard a creak on the stairs and was shocked. Was that Ruth? She will not come in now? I summoned up my courage and went to the door, just waiting to be called back. But the officer did not care about me and I went outside. I turned around briefly; saw that I was not pursued and went quietly to one of the two hiding spots. Ruth was not there and I feared for my big sister.

She must be in the other bedroom, I thought and tiptoed into the opposite direction. Without making a noise I opened the door and walked into the living room. Immediately I noticed that the door to the bedroom was open. I was scared shitless: a soldier stood there, a Tartar or Mongol, who had his machine gun ready aiming at Ruth. He had a big fur hat, a scarred face, unshaven and dirty. He yelled at her and motioned her to come out and lie on the bed. I could do nothing there on my own so I ran back into the kitchen as fast as I could to get Mum. Naturally the officer came running as well and sent the other soldier away before he could do any harm to my sister. I thought he wanted her for himself and I was still very scared. Luckily nothing happened.

Ruth was shivering and her face was pale. When it was over she told us how she had been found. The old Krause had a couple of empty wine bottles hidden behind the sofa, and when the soldier entered the room with his heavy boots, the floorboards moved a little and the bottles collided. The Russian had a closer look and discovered Ruth right there. For safety reasons, we cleared away the bottles.

The times were very uncertain in the spring of 1945 and our neighbours, the Jungfer's, were back in Heidau after their flight. Hilda came to see Mum and wanted to borrow me for a day and a night to visit her relatives in the village of Panten, who were kept prisoners at a Soviet unit and had to look after a large estate there. I suspect the Jungfer family had already been there before, as Hilda knew of the military barriers along the way. Mum was hesitant, because the Russians had just left our property. She did not want to let me go and I still cannot say exactly why she agreed to it in the end. Perhaps Hilda had begged her so much that she could not help it. We went that morning, after I had fetched my jacket. Hilda was about thirty-five, and came with empty hands. She had a plan: I should assume the role of her daughter and deceive the patrols. We went off in a northerly direction, selecting unpaved roads and came through deserted villages. It was a hard road for me but for Hilda with her mobility problems, it was worse. She had one leg shorter than the other one. Bravely and without a pause, she persevered until we arrived at the guarded road block in the afternoon. She was aware that I knew a little Polish, so I did the talking. A sinister-looking soldier asked curtly, 'Kuda?' This is probably 'where to?' I thought and told him that we wanted to visit Hilda's mattka (mother). In reality it was her aunt, but I did not know the right word. It would not have made a difference to the soldier anyway.

'Karasho,' he said aloud, and let us pass. Now it was not far anymore. In one of the workers' houses, we found the family, aunt, uncle, son, two daughters and a small child. Hilda helped in the barn milking and feeding, while I looked around carefully. Then there was a rich evening meal: boiled potatoes with salt, butter and cottage cheese, there was only fresh chives missing. In Heidau we only had potatoes and salt every day. I ate a lot and I washed everything down with a glass of milk. It was dark when I was shown to a room with only one cot in the corner, with a pillow and blanket. Quite strange, I was alone in a strange chamber, the rigors of the day let me sleep without dreams. It was the first time I ever slept alone in a strange bed. I was still thinking how much better a full stomach felt and then I was gone.

The next morning I woke up to the sound of plates and cups in the next room. I got up, folded the blanket, had a short morning toilet under primitive circumstances, and sat down at the table. There we had breakfast with bread, butter and plum jam, served with a little milk! That was more than I had imagined in my wildest dreams and I went for it. We will get nothing for a long time, I thought to myself, and forgot my inhibitions. After the meal we said warm goodbyes with hugs and we were back on the road. We came to the same guard, who recognized us and we were allowed to pass unhindered. Hilda had a little butter and flour with her while I had a bit of cheese. Her little bag was not checked; poor Hilda looked pitiful even to the Russians: small, limping, very thin and a face blackened with soot. I was almost ignored which was fine with me. My big worry was what would I find at home. Would everybody still be alive? The way back seemed somehow shorter.

By late afternoon we arrived at our house in Heidau. With the pre-arranged knock signal Mum opened the kitchen door. 'Thank God,' she said, 'We are all right, Ruth is here, too.' At the same moment we heard the sound of military vehicles coming closer. It was the next convoy, this time much earlier than usual. The reason for this we never knew, of course, as we did not count as people.

A few weeks later, Hilda told us, her younger niece in Panten and mother of the little boy had been shot dead. She was about to give a piece of bread to wounded German soldiers who were released and not fit for transportation to Russia. She was shot in the back through the window of the manor house by a Russian.

The great destruction of Breslau took place on May 6th, 1945. The city had 600,000 inhabitants in peacetime; in the meantime it had grown to one million. People from all directions had sought refuge. The supply of food was very poor, everyone had significant problems. In the mid-14th century, Silesia, and Breslau were part of the Kingdom of Bohemia. They were made part of the Holy Roman Empire. At that time the Jagiellonians ruled the city before it fell later into the hands of the Austrian Habsburgs by heritage contract. After the First Silesian War in 1742 Archduchess Maria Theresa as Queen of Bohemia, gave most of Silesia to the Kingdom of Prussia. Various industries such as chemical and metal production came in around 1850, the province of Lower Silesia was founded in 1919, and Breslau was declared capital. The German Empire seized to exist. Breslau is situated on the Oder River and its four tributaries south of the Cat Mountain Range. The city is located between large numbers of channels and spread out over twelve islands which are actually connected by 112 bridges.

In late 1944 Hitler had declared Breslau a fortress although the defenses had not been renewed since the beginning of World War I. Some refugees left the city in time, for many it was too late. The German troops were exhausted and no longer able to withstand the onslaught of the Soviet dominance. Gauleiter Hanke, who was governor and commander, did not surrender quickly enough so more people died than necessary. Seventy percent of Breslau was destroyed and there were over 200,000 victims.

It was May 8th, 1945. I do not know if anyone in my area knew the date, certainly not me. We were completely out of time and I thought the nightmare would never end and we would have to live as captured outlaws until our last day. We were told by a Russian veteran that the war was over. He served as commander, lived in our house and was being looked after by the Ukrainians. His unit in Heidau had probably given him this information. This veteran shouted, 'Gitler (Hitler) kapuut, voina (war) kapuut!' and we had to congratulate him, and alas, you'd better make a happy face!

For the first time we saw him drunk. I was more afraid of the old Krause than of this Russian. He had never harmed us, yet he was a person of respect and it was not to be trifled with him. He had a gun and we did not want to test his patience.

We kept using Neumann's outhouse and used book pages as toilet paper. The house was on the other side of a dangerous road we had to cross. Small businesses were done in a bucket. Later, my mother cleaned up an outhouse at one of the workers' homes on our property, which we then used. When Ruth had to go, she checked carefully to see if anyone was near because rapes were still happening. Maybe two weeks later, Ruth looked out of the window on our first floor, and saw a convoy approaching on the road from Parchwitz and turn into our private road. Coming closer, she saw some fifty women who walked two-by-two in procession. At the top and at the end of the train was a carriage, each pulled by small horses. Every carriage was manned with three Russian soldiers with machine guns. The girls were at the age of eighteen to twenty-one years in tattered clothes, most of them barefoot and completely exhausted. Upon arrival some sat on the bare ground in the courtyard, two girls lay on the ground, others tried to take care of them.

It was toward the evening and the soldiers ordered the girls to go into one of our barns, which were now almost empty, because all the rabbit furs had been stolen by the Soviets. Two Russians came upstairs to us, while Ruth had already gone into hiding, and seized Grandma Pauline's living room. They moved the table into the middle of the room and ordered us to get out. Our bedroom was located behind the living room and we joined Ruth, who had her hiding spot there. That night I will not forget for as long as I live: the soldiers brought four girls upstairs, gave them some food to eat and alcohol to drink. I do not know if they were forced to drink alcohol or if they drank it voluntarily, because they knew what would happen. We heard singing from the living room, then bawling and screaming. A girl screamed, 'You pig, you're breaking my back!'

They were girls of the Labour Service, who had no chance to escape. The rapes were endless, and we had a mortal fear that our door would be opened. Eventually, it was quiet and I fell asleep shivering. We did not come out until the following morning, when Mum gently opened the door a crack and saw no one lying around drunk anymore. The living room was in quite a mess, it smelled of stale sweat and booze; I did not want to touch anything. On one side there was Pauline's sofa. The girls had come out of the fortress Breslau and had been on their way to Liegnitz. They were then deported to Siberia just like Dad. Anita Pohl, daughter of the master roofer from Parchwitz, was also sent to icy Siberia.

Except that the war was over, we knew next to nothing of the rest of Germany. Returning refugees said they had heard only rumors. One of those rumors which I can remember was that the

Chinese would come and marry German women. There were hair-raising stories, and we never knew how much truth was in them.

-11-

The Hit in the Face

In May 1945 a Polish family of ten people picked Dittrich's house and settled there. Mr. Dittrich showed them how to run the farm. They must have been city dwellers and had to learn everything. I remember that strawberries were planted which they could not even eat because the new Polish mayor took them all. The three Dittrich daughters had to do the Russian's laundry. They were locked up at work, because the laundry room had access to the food storage. Despite all this, the girls had the courage and made pockets into their garments. That way they stole rice, sugar, bacon and ham in the evenings when they went home.

There was a canning factory in Parchwitz, which no longer produced. There was no harvest and no more supply of cans. In the basement of the factory, however, were thousands of cans stored filled with green beans, celery salad, and kale, of which the celery salad tasted the best. In addition, there was also apple and apricot jelly in bulk. After the factory was abandoned, we went, like many others from the Liegnitz district, and took a couple of cans every now and then.

The cannery was closed to us now and guarded around the clock, so we did not go there any longer. A small group of children picked me up; they all wanted to go to Parchwitz. There were supposedly dried vegetables in the attic of a house in a certain street. I was looking for a burlap bag and went with them. We had a handcart to transport the food back onto which every child would put their bag. By now, we knew Parchwitz very well and found the house we were looking for. As always, one of us went in first to explore the place. People, who had apparently not been disturbed, were coming towards us carrying bags filled with vegetables, and so we climbed up the stairs of the abandoned house. We did not find much left in the attic, so we collected the remains and shared them fairly among us. I figured my share would be sufficient for at least four meals. We grabbed our bags, tied them at the top and went downstairs. Then we packed everything onto the cart and two of us pulled it back to Heidau. I was certainly disappointed by the small amount of food we had gotten, because slowly but surely all the supplies would soon come to an end and I did not know where we could get some more next time. On the way home we met a sixteen-year-old boy from Heidau who also wanted to get dried vegetables from the same house. After we told him there was no more, he turned around and walked back with us.

When we approached our private road that Dad had built and I reached for my little bag from the cart, he suddenly said with a sardonic voice, 'Look, the rich Ingeborg Maiwald is organizing food! Yes, I remember, you and your folks once were eating sausages.'

I quickly replied, 'Oh boy, and now you're eating them?' He reached out and wham, I had his right hand in my face. I grabbed my bag and ran the last eighty meters home. I did not want to tell Mum about it, it did not matter to me, but she greeted me at the door and immediately saw the imprint of all five fingers on my cheek. He had slapped me hard.

'What has happened to you?' she asked anxiously. The boy's name was Hofmann and he was the son of a fieldworker. In the winter of 1944, Hofmann senior had asked for a hundredweight of coal. Dad gave him the coal for free...

The few villagers who had returned to Heidau shared as much as they could. One day a woman we did not know came to us and asked for shelter for the night. She had dinner with us and as usual, we only had potatoes with salt. After dinner she had a bit of a wash with hot water in the hallway and asked Mum for a pair of scissors to cut her nails. Mum gave her our only pair of scissors, of course. The next morning we had breakfast together which consisted of homemade bread with sugar beet syrup and cereal coffee. The woman then grabbed her rucksack in the hall and prepared to leave. Mum asked for the scissors but the woman only shook her head frightened. She did an act in front of Mum and searched her coat pockets. She could not find them there. Mum insisted and told her to open her rucksack which the woman was already carrying on her back. Mum took her arm and pulled her back into the kitchen where the woman opened the rucksack on a chair. It was no surprise for Mum to find the scissors there on top. The woman murmured something about an accident and apologized with a red face, took her rucksack and walked off. Mum put the scissors back into the drawer of our sewing machine without a word.

There was a cucumber sorting place in the village which was no longer in operation, just like all the other businesses in the country. From there we took a lattice frame with a metal mesh home. We still had some old potatoes from the previous year and did not want to waste them. We put the uncooked potatoes into a meat grinder and produced a pulp. Then we poured the pulp onto a clean tea towel and tied it up like a bag. The bag was hung above a bucket to collect the liquid. The starch settled at the bottom of the bucket and in due course the water was drained. Then we dried the starch on the mesh. Several hundreds of pounds were processed that way but the yield was low. The dry starch was then added to soups.

Mum could not sleep anymore and she looked absolutely miserable. I was afraid she would die because she had lost a lot of weight, her cheeks were sunken and her eyes had dark circles. She was sick for many weeks and I was helpless. Friedel Obst, who also had returned, gave her a bottle of valerian drops, and from then on Mum got a little better. In addition, we were no longer alone. Friedel's father, an old farmer, had taken his life during the flight after his wife had died. Friedel and her sister Else slept a few nights at our place until they had cleaned up their own house in the neighbourhood.

The Soviets had left the houses in an abhorrent state. There was abandoned furniture, clothes, and all sorts of things left behind in an unholy mess. In between that mess was stinking excrement or, to put it more clearly, the Soviets had left their shit in every room. Everything had to be thoroughly cleaned and washed. Our office looked the same, so none of us had any identification papers, or had Dad burned them before the Russians came? Anyway, I know that he had burned a picture of Hitler that every household and every office had to have, and his uniform in the factory, before the Russians arrived.

It's probably now the time to write a little more about Hans Krause. I'm not sure how to describe this monster. He was about seventy years old then, tall and obese with a comparatively small bald head and a big belly. His trousers did fit, so he must have had the same size before the war. Later in the summer of 1945, they were really loose when his belly was gone. We were told to call him Grandpa Krause and we did. He was something of an appendage of Grandma's. As we detected his treachery, we named him "Box" among us, like a boxer dog. Ursula and I were not allowed to touch his desk which was in my grandma's living room and had an enviable number of green, sharp pencils lying in an elongated case, lined up like soldiers. Krause began to harass us after Dad had been taken prisoner. He sent us for wood and water, which was always a major operation.
'Hurry Ingeborg, no wood, no coal!' he shouted.
Ruth was to fetch water but Mum went instead, because Ruth still had to be hidden. He did not give up on Mum.

The fountain was in the garden, where we could draw water with a bucket, which was attached to a flagpole. The bucket was moved back and forth, and sometimes it just fell into the water and needed to be caught again. When it touched the ground we had to wait until the water calmed down and became clear again.

Since we had a water tap in the house, the well had not been used until after the invasion.

Mum and many others from Heidau worked on the fields. They had to do all the work so the Russians had enough to eat. She told me to go to the military unit at the Pirl Estate and peel potatoes where several German women were preparing soup. I used to go there for quite some time. The German fieldworkers from the village ate with that company at the same table. I also got soup and a piece of bread for my work. Krause was chopping wood there to earn a meal. One day he came home staggering with blood running down his face. Without saying a word he went slowly to his room. We heard from other labourers, that he had stolen a loaf of bread and had been beaten up pretty bad, after he was caught.

We had no central heating, but big heaters in the rooms. Downstairs and on the upper floors there were portable ones which were fired with wood, charcoal or briquettes. I had to get the wood from the goat barn, where the wood for our gas cars was stored and which took up half the room. I always clattered the buckets when I went to the barn, since I had seen a rat scurry past some time before. The coal was carried by Mum; it was too heavy for me and was kept in the unlit basement.

-12-

The long Walk

One day in June 1945, the cows were suddenly taken from our barn. Mr. Menzel and Mr. Jungfer, two older men between 60 and 70 years of age, and Ruth were ordered by a Russian unit to drive the cows from the farm for shipment to the east. Menzel's cow remained with the Pole, who now lived at Menzel's house. Ruth was under duress, opposition was fatal. How did Mum feel? I remember how I felt: Dad was first and now Ruth. When will we see them again? Perhaps never.... Then they all went and later that day when it was dark, Mr. Menzel said to Ruth, 'We must not go beyond the Oder River! The bridges are guarded. We gotta get outta here!'

In the last village before the big river, they gave each other the prearranged signal. Ruth should be hiding in the ruins of a house in search of a supposedly lost cow whilst the men would disappear into the darkness. It was a terrible feeling of doing something forbidden, with the prospect of being shot. It was a risky plan, but all three were determined and did not think twice. There was no shortage of houses in ruins and they waited for the right moment. Luckily, they wore nothing white, which could have been seen despite the low light. Now or never, Ruth thought and took all her courage. She ran off into the darkness and hid as previously discussed. Shortly afterwards the two men did the same thing, they crouched and waited. The next few seconds was the difference between life and death. Their disappearance was not yet noticed. The whole group passed, the clouds did not move, and it was really dark. Ruth hardly dared to breathe. There was still no shot, so the other two were not yet discovered either. Then she heard German voices, whispers. Menzel and Jungfer approached her hiding spot and told her to come out quietly. Under the cover of night they turned around and headed home, the plan had worked. Before midnight they reached Heidau.

There were still soldiers stationed at our place, and so Ruth could not come home, but had to sleep at Jungfer's house. The post came two days later and said to Mum, 'Rutka (Ruth) back, make sleep Jungfer.' Mum acted as if she knew nothing about it, but Hilda Jungfer had already told her. It seemed that the soldier had received the message that the cows had arrived at their destination, but three drivers were missing and he threatened us the next morning. We were lucky it was only a threat. Ruth returned home after a few days because the unit was moved to another location. We were happy to see her back without being harmed. Once our house was abandoned by the Ukrainians we moved into our kitchen on the ground floor and Mum gave Krause nothing to eat anymore. As of now he had to take care of himself. Mum cleaned the master bedroom, my two sisters and I slept with her on a mattress in front. The Russians had also left their shit there and it almost ruined the whole room.

A number of Polish soldiers came to Heidau and treated the Germans at their own discretion which was illegal. They appointed themselves as temporary managers and in the summer of 1945 they collected the last sixty residents. Most of them had returned after the evacuation.

We were driven from our home and, on this occasion, we lost most of our previously salvaged belongings. We had no handcart anymore, only a one-wheeler, which was a gift from Karl to Ruth. This green children's cart could carry a weight of fifty kilograms. We also had a makeshift cart that somebody had made out of a pram base. In the tannery, he had found a light timber table top and a couple of ropes, with which he created a platform. Thereupon two jute bags with clothes and quilts were tied. Our hand luggage consisted of a duvet and pillows for everyone, Ursula only had to carry a pillow for she was a skinny seven-year-old. Then Mum and we three children left our house. Already at the beginning of the trail we saw smoke coming from the house of the Tomczak family and there were several dead bodies being carried out. It was a family suicide, which had been prepared by the father. He had given poison to his wife and young children. The dosage he took was too little for him and he survived. His seventeen-year-old daughter Ursula had refused to take the poison and now they both joined our group. Mr. Dittrich still had two goats but before the expulsions a couple of Poles took the animals away. They looked mainly for small farms and settled down. We were ordered to spend the next two nights in Upper Heidau on a large meadow. Hans Krause stayed home for a little while longer. With the help of his Polish language skills, he had assured the authority that he had Polish ancestry and wanted to stay. Later he had to follow us, no exception possible. He had built himself a cart out of the front suspension of our beautiful carriage and strapped his bags of clothing and bedding to it.

A young Polish soldier, a guard, saw me in the crowd and said I was his sister. In fact, he showed me and Mum a photo of a girl in a communion dress that looked very similar to me. What would happen now? He took me by the hand and led me away. I got scared. To my surprise, in this rainy night I was allowed to sleep with the older people in the nearest house, while all others were camped on the lawn. With the permission of the guards, Inge Hauke, Ilse Grosser and I were able to go back to Dittrich's house again and fetch the last dried vegetables. I do not remember the other nights during the march to the village of Wolfshayn so well. It all went without any extraordinary occurrences. Wolfshayn was located west of Heidau. We got nothing to eat. Mum had some residual self-baked bread and a piece of bacon of perhaps 500g hidden in the luggage. In an abandoned castle in Wolfshayn there was a large, well-equipped kitchen. Mum looked around and found a beautiful teapot, which she pocketed quickly. We did not have permission to go into the other rooms and camped in front of the castle. Calling it camp is an exaggeration. We had not much left and we sat down on the grass. Fortunately it was summer and the night was not too cold. I was tired and soon fell asleep and I'm not sure if Mum slept well. The next morning I woke up with a wet face and noticed water in a trough on the duvet. During the day it dried again and we were always sitting on our stuff because we did not want to lose any more. The next night we were allowed into the castle, where Mum made up a little room for us.

On the third day we saw a herd of cows coming toward us. They were driven by Ukrainian women and they seemed to have problems with the animals. I could not hold back and gave them a hand. It did not take long and the cows came to a halt. We found an old centrifuge on the premises and the women with the cows made milk and cream. One of them gave me a full glass of cream which I wanted to share with my family. The woman did not let me go until I finished the cream by myself. I believe that she did not want to lose the glass.

We also went into a nearby forest and came back with blueberries. In the castle's basement we found potatoes so we had another meal: pancakes with blueberries. Then we waited for the next orders.

'Where will they take us?' I asked myself and there was no answer. Every day we were hungry and falling asleep at night was next to impossible. After a week there was an unexpected turn of events. The guards were gone when we woke up in the morning. What was that supposed to mean? There was silence. We looked around us, but there were no guards watching us. After a brief discussion, the Heidau people decided to go back home. Nobody needed to encourage the others; no one took command. When everyone had packed their bundle, the group gathered, and we left the castle. There was not a single vehicle in sight that we could have used. We first walked on a road, but the majority of our journey was the Autobahn (highway) from Bunzlau to Liegnitz. It was a march of sixty kilometers, the longest walk of my life. Left and right of the wide road there was an unusual emptiness. In the meadows, there were no cows and no sheep. Even the birds had left the area and so the day was very long and painful for all of us.

It was hot and we had neither water nor food. Hour after hour, we walked without speaking towards Liegnitz, with blistered feet, scarred hands, and back pain. I had some very bad shoes which I took off at times, but that was no improvement.

We went without rest because we feared that if we did we would not get up again. Even now no one took the lead. We all knew what was at stake and no one grumbled or complained. Some had reached the point where they were indifferent to whether they would arrive alive or not. We never talked about it and so we walked, meter by meter, on the hot and seemingly endless road. Along the way we found a few green apples, which were quickly eaten. However, this was a mistake, the people in question got diarrhea and lost even more fluid. The oldest among us were doing their best, dragging themselves with their last bit of energy to our destination. Some people of the group spent the night in a village before coming to Liegnitz, whereas we teamed up with our neighbours who had become our friends.

As newcomers to the Heidau community our parents had no contacts. Apart from the mayor Gruhn, Mr. Köhler and the Just family they knew no one. We hurried the rest of the way, so we would come home before nightfall. We feared the raids.

Dead tired, we arrived in Upper Heidau and were taken up by the Rauer family, who provided shelter for the night in their house. They showed us upstairs where we settled down on loose straw. I do not know why the Rauer's had been allowed to stay home in the last couple of weeks.

I could not stand on my legs any longer and collapsed from fatigue. Mum came with a plate of homemade pasta and baked fruit that Mrs. Rauer had prepared. I could not eat anything because of exhaustion, my head was spinning. I just wanted to sleep. Forget the pain. Sleep.

The next morning we went to our house and found it almost destroyed by the Russians. We were used to a lot, but this sight put us in a silent rage and made us almost burst with anger.

Fortunately, our furniture was still there. At that time our house was inhabited only by us and Krause. We spent the days in our kitchen on the ground floor, where also the Göbel and Gerschel families later cooked. The Göbel's moved in with us when they had to evacuate their home making room for a Russian unit.

Our neighbour Ida Ernst had her head shaved because of lice. She had been lying in bed with Ruth's mattress in front of it. Ida used to always comb her hair while sitting on the bed and so it happened that Ruth got lice as well. Mum had saved a dust comb from the factory and Ursula Baumert tirelessly combed her long hair until she had removed over a hundred of these pests. Ursula had her own sense of humour. Mum had gooseberries once and Ursula said, 'Do you shave the gooseberries now and sell them as grapes?'

-13-

The Jelly and the Dungeon

One evening, a Russian officer inspected the first floor of our house and chose grandma's sofa in the kitchen for sleeping. We left him alone and went into our bedroom. The next morning he was gone and we found torn wrapping paper on the kitchen floor. Mum went down on her knees in front of the sofa and immediately checked the underside, where she had hidden a bundle of fur for a coat and a bag of sugar. The officer had found everything and took it with him; surely he must have felt the difference in the suspension. These guys obviously had been in a lot of houses and knew the general hiding spots.

The news spread like wildfire: a horse lay in a ditch, it was injured and had to be killed. Mr. Gerschel and little Ursula immediately went there. I was out organizing something else and came home before them, so I saw them both coming. Each of them had a horse's leg shouldered, not much else was left. It was a funny scene to watch, especially because the horseshoes were still attached and blinking in the sun. Ursula was very proud that she could contribute something to the family and showed us the leg with a smile. Mr. Gerschel said, 'I'll take off the skin and bring the meat into the kitchen.' He went to our barn, where the wood was chopped and took care of the two legs. Ruth took the big beautiful bowl of meat and bone and began immediately with the preparation. She skillfully cut the meat from the bones and cut it into bite-size pieces which she then poured back into the broth. After a while she put everything into a big white enamel bowl for our now eight-person household, and slowly we saw the jelly develop. We could not wait and we checked every five minutes to see if it was ready to eat. I can still see the aspic with chopped fresh parsley and carrot in front of me. All of a sudden there was a knock and Mum went quietly to the front door. She heard sounds in German and asked who was there. Two German soldiers answered, asking if they could stay with us for the night. Mum opened the door and led the two men into the kitchen. They were exhausted and dirty with dry blood on their coats. They asked for some bread, and while they were eating, one said to the other that it would be fantastic to have some horse meat with the bread. Mum, who had not yet touched Ruth's cooking, took the full bowl and placed it in the middle of the table. Stunned, I watched as our food disappeared in no time until the last piece was gone. They ate it all. The family had gotten nothing but apparently it tasted wonderful.

One soldier said his home was on the island of Rügen and they both wanted to cross the Neisse River at Görlitz in Saxony. Mum immediately sat down and wrote a letter to Muttel and Aunt Frieda. She gave the two a few Reichsmarks in the hope they could buy stamps after they crossed the border. Well fed, they were on their way before it got dark in order to find another night's lodging with breakfast since our bread was eaten.

In the summer of 1945 all the good furniture was taken from our home and loaded onto waiting trucks in our yard. The Russian soldiers said Mum could have the furniture returned when the unit would move out of the Pirl Estate. They took heavy oak furniture from the dining room and the master bedroom, the grand piano, the music box and the radio. We had to carry our best porcelain plates and cups to the milk can ramp. It was still sitting there for a while after the furniture had been taken, and Mum then got a few things back into the house, especially the expensive porcelain dancing figurine that used to have its place on the sideboard. The paintings were already gone with the furniture, as well as the electric stove. Clocks were no longer there anyway. The wardrobes were taken, too. The machines in the factory were also removed. Mum and a neighbour brought some electric motors into the house and hid them in the large oven, where the bread was usually baked. Our beds, the kitchen cabinet and a table with chairs were left with us. As the rumors grew that we would leave our home, Mum took the preserve cooking pot, with which she had made jam and preserves before, and put the figurine and a few expensive pieces in it and together we let everything disappear in the pond after dark, hoping to find them again someday.

The Pirl Estate

In the autumn of 1945, Friedel Obst came running and said, 'Klara, the Russians are leaving the Pirl Estate. We can go and get our furniture back!'

Mum grabbed her jacket and went with her so as not to miss anything. It was noon on an overcast day and the Pirl Estate was just a short walk of seven minutes away. We children stayed home and waited for their return. Ursula sat at the window and played with a few rubber bands, which she took from a jar, always keeping an eye on the road. Two hours later there was no sight of the two of them. We were concerned, of course, and I wanted to go and find out where they were. Ursula got up without hesitation and said firmly she wanted to go with me. Without further ado, we were on our way. Ruth stood at the window and waved us goodbye. After a few meters, we walked around the corner and were now on our own. I would rather have chosen a secret path, but we had to stay on the official way, in case they came back. I was not feeling my best. When we arrived there we stopped in front of the large open gate and had a look around. We knew the yard well and we also knew where the various buildings were located. Now we saw three Russian military vehicles sitting there and we were too scared to enter the estate. Where were Mum and Friedel? The hours passed - we heard no unusual noises and waited anxiously. It was cool and it would not be long until dark. Suddenly we heard several gunshots and they scared us to death. Some rounds hit the wall not far from us. Why were they shooting? Even before we could think about it, Friedel appeared breathlessly in front of us and pulled us out of the firing-line. Now we had the answer, they had tried to kill HER!

Luckily Friedel was unhurt, she took us by the hand and we all hid in the next yard behind a wall. That farm was deserted, the family had fled months ago, and there were no troops. When we got settled in that hiding place, she told us still trembling, that she and Mum had been captured and both were locked in a cellar. Down there they sat in a corner and prayed together with soft voices. Again and again, an officer arrived with a bottle of brandy in one hand and a pistol in the other and yelled at them. After a few minutes he went back upstairs and locked the cellar door. They continued praying while they waited in a dark corner, terrified.

Friedel was interrogated several times by the soldiers in an upper room, but without result, because she knew no Russian at all. Mum was still imprisoned in the cellar and up to this point had not been questioned yet. Friedel managed to escape when the interrogating officer was talking incoherently and was so drunk that he dropped his head on the table and apparently fell asleep. At that very moment she took a chance and ran out of the room and down the hall without looking left or right. It was shortly after she left the house, when she heard the gunshots and ran as fast as she could in a zigzag to the gate, where she found us to her surprise. Which of the soldiers had fired she did not know, of course, and it made no difference. The important thing was that she had not been hit and the three of us were safe for the moment. The question now was, what should we do, how could we possibly help Mum?

We waited until sunset. Certain unrest ensued, at that same time we were also becoming more conscious of our helplessness. I crept to the gate and peered around the corner. Right at this moment, something happened in the yard of the Pirl Estate: the engines were started, the soldiers boarded the vehicles with their weapons and drove down the road toward Parchwitz. Then I saw Mum left alone in the last light of day. I immediately reported back and together we ran to her. She had a nasty head injury and blood ran down her face. I was terribly shocked and wished that it was all a bad dream. Ursula and I took her left and right hand, and so we all hurried back home. We did not care about the lost furniture anymore and when we reached our property, we were overjoyed. Once again, they did not get us!

Mum's wound was immediately treated by us and we made a makeshift bandage. The drunken officer had interrogated her and just like Friedel, she knew no Russian. This had made him so angry that he struck at Mum's temple with his gun muzzle. She could have easily died because of that blow and we could not really believe until the next day, how lucky she had been. The scar on her head was a silent witness to this senseless act all her life.

We managed to move around the village with less fear some time later, perhaps we only imagined it this way because we had become accustomed to many dangers. We children went together. We explored the nearby forest south of Heidau to see what it had to offer and we came across a patch of yellow boletus. To be sure, we picked a few and went back home to have them checked. The Göbel women knew all about mushrooms as opposed to Mum and gave us positive confirmation that they were edible. So we went back into the forest and each one of us collected full basket, and immediately the question arose, what to do with this blessing. There was a rumour circulating that there was a black market in Liegnitz and we wanted to sell our treasures there. We discussed what we should buy for it and it turned out that cooking oil was the first priority.

Next morning Liesel, Frieda Göbel and I got ready to find the market in Liegnitz. It was half past nine, and the very first Russian truck stopped to take us. We climbed onto the empty truck bed and sat down. We were not too afraid of possible rapes anymore, since they were prohibited now and we were not in the vulnerable age group. We reached Liegnitz and the truck pulled up in front of a depot, where the driver stopped and we got off. The two Göbel's looked around puzzled and tried to figure out where the market could be. As a precaution, we had covered our baskets with tea towels. We walked down the street and Liesel asked an older man for directions. He looked at us briefly and gave information in German. After a while we found a big public place, and about thirty people talking with each other. We could not discover any goods for sale, however. Had the man lied to us? Or were we at the right place and the goods were hidden? Most shop windows were smashed or shot; all the houses looked very worn. Now and then there was a repaired window and we saw poorly fitted shelves. The three of us stood there helpless like unsuspecting sheep with Polish mumbling around us, which I did not understand. Suddenly there was a warning yell, and they all ran away, only we stayed because we were too scared to run. Armed militia came with fierce looks toward us; an escape was no longer possible. They said, 'Illegal!'

We had to remove the towels from the baskets and the baskets were immediately taken off our hands. All the mushrooms were seized, it was all for nothing. But the case was not over. The two women had to go along with the men, I ran after them until we reached the Polish command post. I was not allowed to go with them and they disappeared inside the building. I was alone and frightened in a strange city in front of a building and did neither know what was happening to the women nor what I was supposed to do. I waited and walked up and down a bit without losing sight of the building. Perhaps there was a back door, where they could take them away?

The hours went by and I was terribly hungry, but I think my fear was even bigger. Very few people went past and no one spoke to me or took notice. I only heard Polish sounds, no German. We had arrived in Liegnitz about half past ten and now it was getting dark. I would not get any food here, should I just try to find my way home? I could not remember the exact way into the city for there were simply too many roads and junctions. I had to quickly find the right way if I wanted to be back in Heidau before midnight. The sixteen kilometers would still be long enough.

I had just started walking a few steps when I suddenly heard my name called from behind and I turned around. It was Frieda. She came up to me alone and I was more than relieved to see her, but at the same time, I worried about Liesel. Together we waited for a while near the headquarters but Liesel did not show. I did not know what to do and Frieda said we should go home for we could not stay there. She knew the route back and so I was spared a lot of detours.

Twinkling stars were already above us and it was night when we finally returned home. To our surprise it did not take too long and Liesel also arrived, we were happy and tired at the same time. Frieda had emptied a sewage pit with bare hands the whole day through, while she was insulted and called 'German pig'. All along the way home I had been wondering about the strong odour, but had said nothing. Liesel had been arrested and was forced to do the laundry with a washboard all day. Since they had been taken to different locations in the building, neither one knew of the whereabouts of the other. They never got anything to drink or eat, but they came back alive.

Mrs. Gerschel, now nearly seventy years old, thought up a plan to acquire food in September of 1945. She poured a liter of apple juice into a saucepan and put on the stove. Then she added a good dose of pepper, industrial salt and who knows what else. After the brew had cooled down, she ran it through a metal sieve and filled an empty liquor bottle. Then she pushed a cork so deep into the neck that it was leveled with the neck opening. Now it was impossible to open the bottle with bare hands. She told me to fetch the handcart and at that moment I saw her hiding the bottle under her worn jacket. She did not say anything and I did not ask. We took the handcart and an empty bag and made our way to Parchwitz. It was an overcast day and we made good progress. Then I realized that she turned off the main road towards the cannery and I got a pretty strange feeling in my stomach. We went straight to the guard at the gate who instantly aimed at us with his automatic gun. Mrs. Gerschel did not speak Russian at all but she made gestures with her hands and pointed to the bottle she had brought along. The guard had a quick look around and accepted the bottle thinking, of course, it contained liquor. Now I understood: the cork in the bottle was sitting so deep that he needed a corkscrew or something similar, to open it. For this he had to leave his post, which was not allowed, naturally. Since he could not open the bottle straight away the deceit would not be detected. That would give us enough time to go into the cellar to fill the bag with cans and pass the guard on our way out. That moment I admired Mrs. Gerschel: what a cunning plan! We left the cart at the stairs, went down into the basement and filled the bag. This time we did not sort the cans by their content, so that even the unpopular kale was thrown into the bag. Then we went back upstairs and loaded our booty into the cart. All this took only a few minutes and we pulled the cart back towards the gate. So far, so good. When we arrived, we saw that the soldier just had opened the bottle and was taking a generous sip. He'd got it open faster than we thought! On cue, we began to run and it was not a second too soon. The guard spat and cursed, and then I heard the bottle hitting the ground. At this moment I thought that in the next few seconds I would catch a bullet in my back and be all over and done. One more step and another one. Mrs. Gerschel ran right beside me with the cart rumbling in the middle. She gasped loudly, 'Run, Ingeborg, run for your life!'

Still no shot yet; I must not stumble, I thought. We kept running and managed to get around the next corner. So far everything went well and we slowed down until we stopped for a short while and listened. It was quiet and it seemed as if he was not following us. We would have heard the heavy boots on the tarmac. We carried on walking and recovered from the sprint. We returned unscathed to Heidau with our goods and we were more than happy. Today, I'd say it was an unforgettable adventure, back then it was normal. We wanted to survive, and we had to take risks. Mum took to the fields at night with other women in order to steal back potatoes. The fields had been acquired by Poles and nobody had any compunction about stealing from them. One must not get caught!

It got colder in October, the winter was near. We did not have a supply of petroleum and did not want to sit in the dark. One morning, Siegfried Göbel, Inge Hauke, Ilse Grosser and I set off towards Parchwitz. I was wearing a gray wool hat and my only jacket, the other children were dressed similarly, and no one had good shoes anymore. We ran a detour to Parchwitz and only used the back lanes. We did not run into checkpoints, not even other people. After an hour we saw the barn, the objective of our journey and our pace slowed. It was surrounded by a fence and guarded by Russian soldiers. The barn was a former storage house of the Wehrmacht and was filled with many barrels of engine oil. Each one of us had brought along a tin can and together we crept up behind the bushes alongside the fence. There we took cover and watched the guards. Since none of us had a watch, we counted the seconds they needed to take a lap around the barn and we noticed at the same time that the lock was broken on the barn door. The guards walked one behind the other and when one disappeared behind the barn, the other one came into sight. That made the whole thing much more difficult for us. We went crouching along the fence and found indeed a hole in it directly above the wet grass. The right moment came and twelve-year-old Siegfried did not hesitate at all. He pushed his oil can through the hole and followed. When one guard turned his back towards us and took two more steps before he disappeared behind the barn, the brave Siegfried ran off. He reached the big door and squeezed himself through the gap. The second guard came around the corner at this instant. Siegfried filled his can, still no sound. When the two guards did the next lap, I slipped off as the next one, and Siegfried came running towards me and disappeared through the fence. Everything went like clockwork with extreme exertion and caution. I reached the barn and pulled the big door back without closing it. We were lucky it was still well greased and hardly made a sound. Immediately, I saw the barrel that lay horizontally on a stand and placed my oil can right under the opening. Then I went over to the other end and lifted the barrel. It was very heavy for me and slowly the oil flowed out. After a moment I stopped and put my finger into the can. I touched the oil and figured that I had enough. Then I quietly walked back to the door and waited until I saw the next girl start running. When the right time came I also ran and left the door ajar. We girls silently saw into each others eyes for a second while we were passing and then we disappeared again, each at her destination.

When the last girl came back and everyone had filled their can, we paused for a moment feeling proud, especially because we had tricked two armed soldiers. I began to breathe normally again and after a quick hand signal we were on our way home. As before, we preferred the back lanes through the fields to the main road. At home we had to make up suitable lamps. We took a mason jar and filled it with oil. Then we punched a hole into a tin lid with a knife and went in search of a wick, which we found in our best carriage. We cut off the braided strap which had been used as a door handle, and slipped it through the hole in the lid as a replacement wick. Now we had light, but because it was not the right oil to burn, the walls and ceiling in the kitchen were blackened with soot in a matter of weeks.

It was not until the end of the year before a small shop opened for business. It was the former Habel Inn which was situated on the last bend toward Parchwitz. We could not buy anything there, because we did not have valid money since Polish zloty had replaced our Reichsmarks and there was no place to exchange them.

It was getting colder and I had no proper coat; the jacket I had was too thin for these temperatures. I thought that I should have a look around the tannery; perhaps I would find some offcuts, which could be made into something warm to wear. I actually found three small goat skins. Unfortunately, it would not be enough for a coat, not even for a jacket. When I showed the skins to Mrs. Gerschel she had an idea: we'll make a cape. From her former grocery store she had a few fashion magazines with patterns. She gave me a wheel tool with spikes and we looked for a suitable size. She also had a razor blade and cut out the templates, which I had transferred from the pattern onto a piece of wrapping paper, also found by Mrs. Gerschel. The weather was bad, and there was nothing to organize (another word for steeling back at the time), so I stitched the pieces together with a strong needle with white thread that had been used in the factory. The backside used up one skin, while we needed the other two for the front. The front closure consisted of a tab on one side and two incisions on the other. The tab was pulled through the incisions and kept it all together. Now I had something a bit warmer to wear over my jacket. My trousers had gotten a little short recently, but they would have to do for the upcoming winter. Being proud of my new garment, I went to get milk with a jug hidden in a bag in the afternoon. It was one of those days where I went to the Menzel's to get milk for Ursula. I had not gone far when I saw a whole group of Polish children came running toward me. The white cape! I quickly turned around and ran as fast as I could back home. I never wore the cape again outside, because I thought they wanted to beat me up and take it away. From then on I only wore it at home, but unfortunately it did not keep me warm as I had expected.

In the autumn of 1945, the Gerschel and Göbel families were living with us. Their homes had been confiscated and we took them in. Mr. Gerschel was very ill and needed care. His wife had been able to save a few interesting things from her mum-and-pop store, of which I will tell you more about later. On Christmas Eve she set up a long table and put Christmas tree candles at each place. She and her husband lived in our former dining room and so we got ready for a meal. The old Krause was also invited, because no one knew of our hostile tension.

We were three families that night, we sang Christmas carols together and we did not forget to include our relatives in our prayers. It was a very sad time for us. We had canned vegetable soup, which we had stolen from the canning factory in Parchwitz, plus home-baked bread. Mrs. Gerschel lit the candles and in the course of the meal Krause's candle died without being burned down. She was frightened and whispered it was a bad sign. Mum told us a little later that she obviously was superstitious.

The Göbel family consisted of two sisters-in-law, Frieda and Liesel. Frieda had a little daughter named Trautel, who was two years older than me, her sister Lena had been killed in Dresden on February 13th, 1945. Over a thousand Allied bombers flew nonstop across the city, and little Lena was one of about 35,000 civilians who did not survive the three massive air attacks. Liesel had two children: Siegfried and the six-year-old Barbara. Furthermore there was old Mrs. Göbel, mother-in-law of the two women whose husbands had both been farmers with their own land.

They all lived in the attic, where we had sufficient furniture. Both families reached us with little luggage as they were forced to leave their homes in great haste. Later in the spring, they were allowed back to their homes and from then on we lived in the dining room and slept in an adjoining room, all four of us in two beds. Although we now had plenty of room in the house, we always slept in one room and always dressed.

Between Christmas and New Year's Day 1945, two former Polish workers came to visit us and to see especially Dad. How disappointed and sad they were when they learned of Dad's fate. They lived near Waldenburg and had taken over an abandoned farm near the village. One of the men was called Bulka and he had married a Ukrainian woman named Anna who also previously had worked for us.

We thought that the Ukrainians would go home, but later we learned that they were transported to Siberia, because they had worked in Germany, thus for the enemy. Anna Bulka, born Trochomenko, escaped this horrible fate by this marriage. She had formerly been a teacher and used to sit at the table in the office when I did my homework. She had inscribed labels of fur samples that were sent for analysis to the Laboratory of Freiberg in Saxony.

The two Poles took me shopping to the little shop that had been set up in the former Habel Inn. They only had little money and so they purchased a piece of butter and a bottle of brandy. After the exceptionally rich dinner in the kitchen, which Krause also attended, the men stayed at the table. Mum and we three children said goodnight and went upstairs to bed. Some time in the middle of the night my mum woke me up and asked me to quietly investigate why it smelled of smoke. With extreme caution I opened Krause's kitchen door, where the two poles were asleep, but saw nothing and went back to Mum. She then sent me up to the attic, where Göbel's bedroom was, again nothing. Then I went on my own decision to Krause's living room door, opened it and immediately I was surrounded by thick smoke. I ran back to Mum, we roused the Poles, who then carried the half-dead Krause out of his room down to the garden. They placed him under the trees and tried to save his life with fresh air and water. The poisoning was already too advanced, and old Krause died shortly thereafter.

Meanwhile, other residents put out the fire, I do not remember who though. I sat with Ursula next to Mrs. Gerschel and wept, not for Krause, but because I was afraid to lose our home. Mrs. Gerschel rebuked me, 'Your grandfather is dying and you are crying about a burning house?' For me there was no question of what was more important.

The next morning, the Polish mayor was informed and he interrogated mainly the two Poles. Mum also was being asked whether the two had something to do with his death. She said no and stated that she had left the men in the kitchen with a bottle of brandy. After the following investigation it was found that Krause had heated a brick on the stove in his kitchen and contrary to his custom it was not wrapped in newspaper. The brick was being used as a foot warmer in bed. Apparently it had been too hot, when the mattress was charred and resulted in thick smoke. He was found leaning against his bed and most likely he had been too drunk to escape.

In January 1946 Mum and I walked in extreme cold to Parchwitz to ask Minister Hirschmeyer to bury Krause. I had no more proper shoes, the last pair that would fit me, had been stolen by a Russian. Now I was wearing a pair of shoes, which were given to me by Mrs. Menzel. They had belonged to her sister from the town of Leschwitz who had died of typhoid fever. They were black with one inch heels and had the thinnest soles I've ever seen. It seemed as if I was walking barefoot, every step was painful. They did not fit properly and were not made for those weather conditions. I got frostbite on several toes that day and they itched for years to come when it was freezing outside.

The old Krause was buried with priestly assistance, after Mum had hired the neighbours Jungfer and Menzel to make a coffin out of a wardrobe from the attic. They also organized the transport to the cemetery. Mrs. Gerschel, as a former shop owner, had a few rarities at hand. She gave me and Ursula black velvet ribbons, which we wove into our braids. Ruth was also offered one, but she did not take it and did not attend the funeral. Ruth said very convincingly, 'If I go to the cemetery, I'll throw a big stone into the grave!'

The men involved were paid by Mum with briquettes. As far as I know it was the only funeral at the time in Heidau in the presence of a priest. Hans Krause had also robbed us. He stole the sum of 20,000 Reichsmarks in cash that Dad had withdrawn shortly before the invasion of Russian troops. Furthermore he took a letter of protection that had been written and signed by our foreign workers. Mum found the money later in the living room oven of his apartment, but the letter was missing and never found.

The Heidau population was protestant with the exception of maybe four families. The cemetery was laid out around the church, where our teacher played the organ. Next to the excavated pit, there were the last three relatives buried by the Dittrich's from the last farm in Heidau and two old people who had recently died from typhoid fever. Two grandchildren survived: a boy and a girl less than ten years of age. They had come to the country because of the bombings in the city, and fortunately they were taken in by the neighbours called Engel. They were then all together driven from their land. The father came back from captivity one day and was able to find his children. He received an affidavit from Mr. Dittrich that his wife had died and he remarried later.

Ruth's friend Ursula Baumert also became ill with typhoid fever and lost her hair after a few weeks. She was very lucky to get well later and her hair also grew back.

In the spring of 1946, there was a butcher and a grocery store in Parchwitz. Mum had asked sick released prisoners of war previously to take a letter to her mother. Now a new post office opened in the old building. Meanwhile returnees told Mum where Muttel and Aunt Frieda were and gave us their address. The fact was, we had to somehow organize new stamps as quickly as possible. Since we had no zlotys Mum gave me Krause's underwear to sell, two vests and a pair of long underpants. This time I walked alone to Parchwitz and went to the butcher shop. I stood at the door so that I had an escape route and presented my barter goods. The butcher's wife took the underwear one by one and checked it thoroughly. She lifted the goods up to determine the size. Her husband was a big strong man, and she thought they would fit. She then gave me a few zlotys. At the post office I had enough money for a stamp, so I mailed the letter. Since not all the money was spent, I decided to buy a box of matches. During this time I went a few more times to Parchwitz by myself and always brought 150ml of cooking oil back home. Once I met Gertrud there who was formerly employed at our factory. Now she worked at an estate in Parchwitz where the new owner was an unmarried Pole and she was his housekeeper. After I had told her what I was doing, she gave me two embroidered white pillow cases for sale. I sold them somewhere, always with my back to the door and always alert, of course. Except for some oil I could not buy anything, so I always took an empty bottle from home. When Hilda Jungfer heard that I had sold old Krause's underwear and got zlotys in return, she wanted to come along on my next selling tour. I agreed and early one morning we walked to Parchwitz because the oil was used up again. For a change, we had made baked potatoes and were down to the last drop. The former butcher Mr. Tilger was gone and the shop was now operated by Poles and I had instant success. The butcher bought probably the last set of underwear I had to sell and I got a few zlotys for it. Hilda offered her brown bridal shoes in several stores, but found no takers. No one was interested in the small shoes and she did not want to give them away for nothing. She feared that they would take her shoes without paying and with that thought she hid her holy memento quickly under her garments. She had married during the war, but unfortunately, her husband was killed in a battle like so many others. I bought my oil, and we went back home unharmed. Every time I stood at the front door, I saw the relief in Mum's face and there was always a hug. I think she was constantly praying! The Polish man by the name of Rospendek asked Mum if she would stay in Heidau. He used to work on our land and had come for a visit.

We supplied the whole Liegnitz District with our industrial salt. I suppose it was no longer chemically treated in the last years of the war, because it did not taste like kerosene or the like anymore, and also we had no more rashes. Mum did not ask for anything in exchange when we were invaded by all the people who came to us with their carts. However, she paid with coal when Ursula was seriously ill and suffered permanent diarrhea for some time.

The cow that was hidden at Menzel's probably did not give enough milk and I was in charge for ten days to organize one liter of milk every evening, so I went through the gardens behind the houses and asked the neighbours. Fortunately the milk helped and my little sister recovered rapidly. It was probably not dysentery, for the rest of us were not affected, which was a miracle in itself after so many months under poor living conditions. Ruth had to suffer heavily, too. This time it was scabies. I remember very well how she sneaked around with a pillow, looking for a chair and carefully sat down. The scabies had attacked her backside and itched terribly. Ruth was more prone to diseases than we were because of her many hiding spots.

Ruth was not the only one with her illness. Her friends Ursula and Hilde also had scabies, which is very contagious. One morning the three of them were on their way to Liegnitz. The road was dangerous. Russian soldiers in trucks still ruled the roads but there were not as many as the year before. Every now and again they fetched young girls at random and raped and beat them. They even took their belongings. After only a short time one of those trucks stopped and the soldiers shouted and waved, inviting them for a ride. The three girls jumped over the ditch in panic and ran into the adjacent field. Fortunately, the truck drove on and the girls could continue their long walk. The weather held up well, it was still cool, but suitable for a walk of this magnitude. They had no food and when they arrived in the city, they found a well, but they could not drink the water without boiling it first. They feared strangers therefore they did not knock on any door and walked on thirsty. Without further interruptions, they reached the house that had been described to them. In front of the house there was already a long line of women waiting. The three girls went up the stairs and stood there, shy and without talking. A young physician's assistant came up to them and asked what they wanted. Ursula and Hilde showed their hands and said they all have scabies. The assistant said with relief, 'Thank God, this is not so bad, wait here.'

He disappeared inside and left the three in front of the door. After a short while he came back and gave them three jars of ointment. The door was open and the girls saw a woman in the hallway on an old stretcher. Apparently all ground floor rooms were occupied. Ruth, Hilda and Ursula knew without further information that they witnessed mass abortions. All the women in line had been raped by Russian soldiers and the three realized once again how lucky they were. Hilde vomited twice on the way home, but since she had hardly eaten anything, it was mostly a painful choking. The way back took a little longer because they were getting tired. They still had to look around and take care just in case there was another military vehicle on the road. The spots infested with scabies were still itching when they arrived in Heidau, all dusty and hungry. Meanwhile it was shortly before dark and the families were waiting anxiously. With a short greeting Ruth ran past us and disappeared into the bedroom. The ointment helped rapidly and was sufficient; there was not another walk to Liegnitz required. The rest of us did not get so sick, that we needed a doctor, but could always cure ourselves with the help of home remedies and old neighbours. The golden rule was that water always had to be boiled in order to avoid typhoid fever or dysentery. We could not brush the teeth for a long time since there were neither toothbrushes nor toothpaste available. At the end of the war there were special stones that one had to rub with a toothbrush to generate some foam.

I missed the school, my friends, and my books. An incredible fear arose: would I stay forever uneducated? My sister Ursula had not even finished the first year at school. I wanted to give her lessons, so I went into the deserted staff room of my old school and looked for some useful things in the chaos in front of me. I needed paper, pencils and textbooks. I was lucky and found a couple of empty exercise books and the aforementioned utensils scattered all over the place. I wrapped everything in a torn down curtain and looked for the best way home. The most important thing now was that I did not get noticed by Polish children with my treasures. I used an old hidden path behind the houses where we had played hide and seek a long tine ago. It seemed like ages now. This time it was not a game, it was serious and I ducked through the gardens and was glad when I eventually got home undetected. I made up my mind to teach not only Ursula, but also other children. Reading, writing and arithmetic were as important as eating to me. For many months I had not slept properly, always haunted by the day's events and I quite often woke up in the middle of the night. Then I looked for Mum and she would try to calm me down.

However, I never got to teach my classes. My possessions arrived intact and I proudly showed them to my family and the Göbel's, whose two children I also wanted to teach. Mum slowed my enthusiasm and told me that as of next morning I would have to herd a neighbour's cows. The little farm had now been taken over by a Polish family, and the new farmer was entitled to boss me around. My project came to an abrupt end. My disappointment was huge and I was afraid to take strange animals in a pasture near the woods. I had to pull them with ropes and cross a road which was busy with military vehicles, and then tie them to the ground a kilometer from our house. The first time the Polish peasant showed me, what I had to do and where the three cows should graze. After the first day it had become so boring that I decided to take Mrs. Göbel's nephew Peter along. After I got permission the six-year-old came with me and I felt better since I had someone to talk to. I told him fairy tales and he listened with interest. Sometimes we sang nursery rhymes and so the days went by a little faster. The Pole gave me bread with butter and a small bottle for lunch, which I shared with Peter. It was not cow's milk but it tasted a bit like clay, so I suppose it was sheep milk. I did not drink much of it, Peter seemed quite fond of it. I stood up straight in the evenings and became my own sundial.

That way, I was able to determine the time because we had to be back on the farm between five and six o'clock.

One day I saw a snake and thought it was a viper. I had never seen one before and got scared. I quickly grabbed little Peter by the hand and together we ran to a spot without grass where we could see if the snake was pursuing us. On that day we did not go back to the cows until home time. We watched them from a distance of fifteen to twenty meters instead.

On another day, in the late afternoon, a thunderstorm moved in and the cows were getting restless. We were already on the way home and I led them with the ropes as always when one cow suddenly broke away and stormed off. I had to let go of the other two ropes and ran after the first one. Shortly thereafter, the other two ran off too, but in a different direction. Peter could not stop them, of course, and stood there in shock. I was terrified that they would all run onto the road. The farmer would probably have beaten me senseless, so I ran for my life. Finally, the first cow came to a halt because the ditch was too big a hindrance. Out of breath I chased them. Finally I got the three beasts back together and delivered them. I was still trembling. Peter caught up with me, but did not say a word. The next day I did not go back there. The Pole came to our place to see what was going on, but Mum saw him first. She immediately knew that he was coming to get me. She shouted out loud, 'Ingeborg, quickly go to bed!'

I ran and jumped into bed with my shoes on, covered myself up to the neck, since I was fully dressed. The farmer was in the house now and I heard Mum telling him, that I was sick. That was my cue and I knew what I had to do. The door was flung open and he stood there at the foot of my bed. Out of sheer fear I did not move and Mum's plan worked out all right. Without a word he left our house. Since that experience I never went again and he never came back. He had probably found another child for the unpaid job.

To find something edible was a daily task and was always difficult. I remember Siegfried looked for swallow nests in the stables and he gave us some eggs.

In the village of Heinersdorf there was now a Polish school, after many people from the eastern part of Poland had been resettled in Silesia. I wanted to go there and learn, but Mum would not let me. A few days later we were expelled and went on our journey into the unknown.

-14-

The Train and the Lieutenant

Only a short time before our departure, we had received orders to go to Liegnitz the next morning. Mum spent the night baking bread and packing our belongings into self-made bags. I will never forget the smell of the fresh bread. The fabric for the bags was taken from an abandoned house. Mum stitched them all together with some black thread.

The order said, we must not take baggage exceeding 20 kgs and only as much as we could carry. Money, jewelry or other valuables were not allowed to be taken. We still had 18,000 of the 20,000 Reichsmarks remaining; mother had always kept the bundle of notes on her body. The money was now hidden in the double bottoms of the hand luggage and in a children's book, which I would carry. The book was titled "Our Girl" and I had found it in the abandoned house of Gisel's family. We prepared glue with flour and water, and then we put a few notes between the pages and glued them together. Whatever money was left got hidden in homemade sanitary napkins which we put into the knickers we were wearing. I had also found Gisel's hymn book and put it into my hand luggage.

I could not sleep well that night and I believe the others felt the same. Every little noise woke me up and I was always ready to jump out of bed. After such a long period of nighttime raids you do develop a sense of impending danger.

On the morning of July 1st, 1946 we had a quick slice of bread with syrup and a cup of coffee from self-roasted cereal grains. Mum opened a can of milk that she had received in exchange for an electric oven from a Polish neighbour. I had mixed feelings and

I was not too well. Saying goodbye to our home was very hard on one hand, but on the other hand I only wanted to get away and leave the misery behind me. I was sad and disappointed about the adult world, but I was also glad to be saved from this nightmare. I had next to nothing left as far as personal belongings were concerned and so I did not have to think about what I wanted to take and what to leave behind. The last thing I had was a silver children's spoon engraved with my initials. I quickly slipped it into my pocket. My thoughts were with my father, who would not know where we had moved to. How was he supposed to find us? Was he still alive? He had told us a long time ago, we should turn to the address of one of his clients in Leipzig in case we got separated. The address was R. Max Schulze, Leipzig, C1, Brühl 68, provided, however, that he still lived there. And what if not?

The thought of never seeing my father again made me almost crazy. I wanted to get rid of that thought, because a life without him was unimaginable for me. It pursued me for a while. Mum talked to me with courage and I knew I could trust her. Our little family was now ready for the journey. One final time I looked back at our house but without tears, none of us cried. I had experienced so much there, we used to play there, and I had seen injustice and death there. I had a lot of questions but no answers. Where will we live? Will the new people be good to us? Can I go back to school? Is there a life without fear? It was very scary to me and my heart was filled with pain.

We commenced our walk to Liegnitz, because Heidau did not have its own railway station. The remaining German population of the village was expelled simultaneously, and so a large group moved west. We chose to put on two sets of underwear each, in order to lighten our load. The handles of the bags cut into my hands, plus I was carrying a cast-iron cooking pot that would not fit into any bag. Since the pot handles were not suitable to be carried for a long time, the pain began immediately. After about two hundred meters, it was too heavy for me and Mum told me to throw it into the ditch. Without thinking I dropped it there and then and felt some relief. Still, I could not imagine carrying the two bags to Liegnitz either. In the left bag, there was a loaf of bread, a plate, a cup, eating utensils, one set of underwear, a blue jacket, and two towels. In the right one I had a rolled up duvet and a pillow with double linen. Mum had already taken out some of the down feathers to make it easier for us. She was carrying a teapot, an embroidered tablecloth, two summer dresses and Dad's white jacket, his last possession. We walked along in silence next to Mum, each one lost in her thoughts. My shoes would not last much longer and I had no idea how I could get new ones. My knees ached, because the night before I tripped and fell in the attempt to get some milk. I was almost caught by Polish farmers and had to flee without milk. It was already dark and I stumbled upon a piece of wall someone had tipped over. With bleeding knees I then took a detour home. I always returned with my heart pounding, when I knocked the pre-arranged signal on the door, and was relieved when my mum opened and I could see that everything was fine.

When we reached the Caspari homestead, a Polish peasant who now lived at Menzel's and managed the farm, said to Mum, that she could load the luggage onto the rickety wooden wagon, which was pulled by a brown horse. The high wagon had been in operation for quite many years, which clearly showed. It had iron-studded wooden spoke wheels, hardly any grease in the hub, and did not look very promising anymore. The Pole then let other families' luggage be loaded as well and we were on our way. We walked behind the wagon and we were glad and thankful that we did not need to carry our bags anymore. We arrived in Liegnitz and came to a halt and unloaded the wagon. We now thought our journey would continue straight away. Far from it, they made us wait outdoors for three whole days on the premises of Melzig's sports shop. It was hot although it rained a lot and we got soaked to the bones for there was not even a roof we could use for shelter.

Dad and I knew Mr. Melzig since we bought the timber off cuts from him to fuel our cars that ran on wood gas. He was a nice, big man but I did not see him in transit. In peace times he used to make leather balls and sport shoes, but he had to change production in the war and manufacture wooden soles. Now the house looked rather abandoned. The three nights we slept on our bags in the open. We had only our dry bread to eat. We were permitted to get drinking water from a well in a nearby backyard. It goes without saying that an armed soldier walked right beside us on these occasions.

On the second morning, while I was standing at the fence I saw the Polish woman who had lived for a few weeks in our house coming down the road. She also saw me and motioned me to come over. To my surprise she gave me a little pack made of wild rhubarb leaf, which I took back through the waiting crowd to my mother. I hid it under my wet jacket for I had learned my lesson. Mum opened it and we did not know what to say: it was half a pound of butter! This was an incredible moment for us because we had not seen butter in a long time. That woman, whose name we never learned, had been brought to us with her three sons, 6, 9 and 13 years old, from the Polish mayor's house. They came from eastern Poland, and had a cow and three chickens. The mayor told us that everything Mum had planted in the garden must be shared with them.

During the nights we were quite often awakened by loud shouting, because Polish gangs tried to steal our luggage. They were driven off with clubs and fists. During the days we repeatedly saw long convoys of Germans passing with similar luggage. Finally on the fourth day we got our marching orders by Polish soldiers and we were escorted out on the road to the station and checked by them. They were looking for valuables in the bags. Just when we got to the railroad tracks, we were searched by Polish militia, but fortunately they did not find anything. Mum had sewn her wedding ring and her golden earrings into the hem of her dress.

The whole group was sent to embark on empty cattle carriages, about thirty people in each one. The Dittrich, Tschäpe and Menzel families were in our carriage and it was quite good that we knew each other. In general, the Heidau inhabitants were welded together by the cruel events of the past. The Caspari family and their maid with a baby were also with us. There were eighty people remaining from the six-hundred and forty inhabitants, which we had in 1939 before the war.

Our special train had to stop often, because regular train traffic was already back in operation. During the waiting periods we were allowed to relieve ourselves. In one of these breaks, Caspari's maid missed to return to our carriage on time. There was a lot of excitement because her baby was with us. At the next stop the mother climbed back into our carriage. She had to jump onto the last carriage at the previous stop and was pulled in by the other passengers. Everyone suffered from dehydration, and some fell asleep from fatigue without moving for hours. It smelled a little of cattle in the carriage but we knew it could not be helped. We wanted to survive. Just survive. We arrived at the town of Kohlfurt and everyone had to get off. Gertrud Schade, one of our former employees, made a bonfire next to the tracks, and we managed to get water in a pot and put it on the flames. In the meantime, Gertrud found wild coltsfoot growing near the tracks and we were able to make some tea. To our astonishment she had saved some sugar and everyone got a little spoonful into the cup. I can imagine that she took the sugar when she was working as a maid in a Polish household before we left. The other houses were empty, and no one else had any sugar.

All displaced persons had to stand in line for registration. If one had a birth certificate, it had to be presented, but most of the people had none. Our family also did not have any and so we just said our names. The registration was carried out by German civilians; British troops were stationed in Kohlfurt and monitored the process. Then we had to face another process: killing lice! It was probably more than inhumane. The heads were dusted with white powder, that already looked very unreal. Then the skirts had to be lifted, and the powder was blown with a blower into the underwear. When it was our turn Mum firmly said, 'We do not have lice and we do not have fleas either!' On that day Mum was on edge. She had been through so much that her patience came to an end. The officer sensed that and did not say anything. Then only our heads were treated. Later we got something to eat: bread and canned meat, and we filled our cups with water. In the evening there was an order to get ready for the onward journey. So we lined up again, while the luggage had been left in the carriage. For some inexplicable reason, someone began to sing the Silesian Song *(Schlesierlied)* and everyone joined in:

Kehr ich einst zur Heimat wieder,
Früh am Morgen, wenn die Sonn' aufgeht.
Schau ich dann ins Tal hernieder,
Wo vor einer Tür ein Mädchen steht.

Kehrreim:
Da seufzt sie still, ja still und flüstert leise:
Mein Schlesierland, mein Heimatland,
So von Natur, Natur in alter Weise,
Wir sehn uns wieder, mein Schlesierland,
Wir sehn uns wieder am Oderstrand.

In dem Schatten einer Eiche,
Ja, da gab ich ihr den Abschiedskuß.
Schatz, ich kann nicht bei dir bleiben,
Weil, ja weil ich von dir scheiden muß.

Kehrreim

Liebes Mädchen, laß das Weinen,
Liebes Mädchen, laß das Weinen sein.
Wenn die Rosen wieder blühen,
Ja dann kehr ich wieder bei dir ein.

English translation:

When I once again return to the homeland,
Early in the morning when the sun rises.
Then I'll look down into the valley,
Where there is a girl in front of a door.

Chorus:
As she sighs quietly, so quietly and softly whispers:
My Silesia, my home country,
Nature's beauty, nature in the old way,
We'll meet again, my Silesia,
We'll meet again on the banks of the Oder River.

In the shade of an oak tree,
Yes, there I gave her the kiss goodbye.
Honey, I cannot stay with you,
Because, yes, because I have to leave.

Chorus

Dear girl, don't cry tears
Dear girl, please don't cry tears

When the roses bloom again
Well, then I will be back again.

After the first verse, we were interrupted by a British lieutenant who spoke to us through an interpreter, 'Stop singing! One does not sing when one is expelled from the homeland!'

We were then too afraid to continue singing. The sudden silence reminded us that we had no rights at all and that we were worthless. The adults were probably hit harder with that comment than the children, it is difficult to assess today.

On the way we passed flagman houses and I saw flowers in their gardens but also red and white flags and yellow and white flags. I was terrified and thought we were still in the new Polish territory. Then I remembered that they were church flags, we had a holiday and it must have been a Sunday. We travelled on the same carriage and reached the town of Uelzen the next morning. Shortly after the train stopped, the doors were pushed open and this time it was a proper train station, therefore the exit was much more comfortable. We all took our luggage and a couple of Germans led us to a refugee camp just outside the town. Previously, the camp had been used as accommodation for foreign workers. It was clean and tidy, the bedrooms were equipped with iron double bunk beds and most importantly, almost luxurious, with showers. Can anyone imagine that? Having a shower after about eighteen months! It was the first shower of my life since I only had bathed before and it was incredible. We discovered bruises and minor cuts, we had not previously noticed. I had felt so much pain in the past few months that I probably paid no heed anymore. Even breathing was easier now; a first, long mislaid sense of security went through my body. I could not completely trust the situation I was in, however, and I remembered my father, whom I had not seen for so long now. Was he all right? He certainly would not have a hot shower and soap. Had he found friends among the prisoners? I was sure that the Russians would treat him badly.

In the town of Dössel, our next stop, Mum made me a summer dress from one of hers by hand. We stayed for a few days, maybe two weeks in a camp, much like an army camp. The long buildings were made of wood and would accommodate several families. The four of us were assigned to a bunk bed in which we had to sleep. There was a dining room where we got three meals a day. There was no meat on the menu, just vegetable soups. The food was never enough for us, we were so hungry that we went to the village and begged for food. We went door to door and asked for fruits or a slice of bread with jam. I was on the road begging with the same children, with whom I had stolen the engine oil from the old barn. This time it was not an adventure, but degrading. I felt bad and had to once again swallow my pride, no matter how small it had become. Once we got a beautiful piece of crumb cake, another time we walked through the fields and saw a farmer cleaning a load of carrots. He gave us three carrots per head, of which I ate one and shared the other two with the family. The weather was consistently good and dry. Our laundry was hanging on the line every day and dried quickly. Every day we would wash our clothes with a small piece of soap in the washroom, since we had nothing else to wear. The days passed and then suddenly we were given a new address. The village was called Rimbeck, which we had never heard of, of course. We grabbed our possessions and got on an open truck to our last stop.

-15-

The Bells of Rimbeck

When we arrived in Rimbeck, which was situated right next to the village of Scherfede, there was only one tiny room for the four of us. Therefore the mayor decided that Ruth had to stay elsewhere and told her to stand in line with other girls. Some women of the village were looking for a maid.

'Do you want the blonde one or the black one?,' Mrs. Bergmann asked her daughter Mrs. Kramer. Ruth was taken by the Kramer's just like a commodity on that day. It was so degrading and today I can still shake my head about it. It was a tragedy that Ruth was separated from us. Since she was seventeen, she was supposed to be glad to get a job. That was the opinion of the Scherfede people anyway. For Ruth, the social decline was almost unbearable and she felt like Cinderella. There was food, free accommodation and some pocket money and she worked in the household of the butcher shop and restaurant, but had nothing to do with customers and guests. Among other things, she had to brush the hair of the grandmother of the house and she hated it. On the other hand, the food was good and plentiful, and she was treated adequately by the other family members. In Heidau she could easily employ several maids, now in Rimbeck she was one herself. Some time later she took the first opportunity to get away.

Mum, Ursula and myself were sent to the blacksmith Wilhelm Laudage, opposite the church in Rimbeck, house number 5. Mrs. Laudage was very surprised that there were three of us, for she had expected only one person. Ruth could not stay with us because the room was too small at Laudage's house. She could not forgive Mum for a long time that Mum did not protest.

The Laudage House 1946

Mrs. Laudage wore mourning clothes. In April 1946, her eldest son Hubert had passed away being only nineteen years old. He contracted rheumatic fever during his deployment at the Reichsarbeitsdienst RAD (Labour Service) and still had to continue working until his heart was badly damaged. Then he was sent home and was so weak that he could no longer carry his bag. Soon after, his short life came to an end with severe pain.

The daily life got a little better for us. Mr. Laudage used to clean the barn, where he kept a cow and a pig. The Laudage's had three more children, Franz, 15, Bernhard, 17, and Elisabeth, 12, like me. Franz was an apprentice at his dad's smithy. He had finished business school, but after Hubert's death he worked with Mr. Laudage. Bernhard was being taught to become a carpenter at Mr. Gieseler's workshop.

Some families from Heidau now lived in Rimbeck, and the rest were spread out all around Warburg. None of my friends from home had come to Rimbeck. At least Ruth had her friend Gerda Dittrich close by. I only saw the boy again in Rimbeck, who I had been tutoring in Heidau.

Elisabeth Laudage in 1946

Mum made herself useful at Mrs. Laudage's household from the first day. She washed the dishes and asked what else had to be done. She never was a woman who would sit around and do nothing. She always worked hard and she could not and would not change that now.

The first thing I heard from Laudage's daughter Elisabeth was, that the summer holidays had just started and I would have to wait four more weeks until the beginning of the new term. Believe it or not, I was disappointed and thought it was an eternity until then. I could not wait to learn something new and lead a somewhat orderly life again. We both got along very well right from the start, which means that from then on we were working together and did all sorts of tasks. Since Mum took over some of Elisabeth's work, my new friend was more outside than before and thus I had the opportunity to become acquainted with my new environment. She had invoices to deliver at the end of the year, for all the magazines and newspapers from church. No matter what was collected, it was Elisabeth's task and I went with her. Every Saturday afternoon we swept the street and then we cleaned the shoes for the whole family. Mr. Laudage rang the bell at church and when the three bells were needed, we girls helped him.

From mid-August until the autumn holidays I went to the school in Rimbeck fifth grade and Ursula also went back to school. She was eight years old now and had to start again in the first grade which she did not like, because she was amongst six-year- old children. That was pretty boring for her and not much fun. She could still remember everything she previously learned and she thought it was unjust, of course. As the teacher Mr. Schmücker did not help me when the school started, Elisabeth taught me fractions which she had known since Easter. Then I met Zita, the daughter of the park ranger Mr. Fischer. She was in the first year in high school at the 'Poor School Sisters of our Lady' in Warburg. We spent the autumn break gathering beechnuts. Thank heavens, in 1946 and 1947 there were so many of them that we had enough oil made for us.

I begged Mum to enroll me in high school which seemed impossible, because we did not have the money for it. Mrs. Laudage organized Mrs. Zislawkowski to give me private tuition in English. I had to make up for the first half year. She did not take money for it, although Mum offered to pay. I'm not sure if I had four or five lessons, but I remember it did not take too long.

After the autumn break of 1946 I went to high school in Warburg, Westphalia! I had pressed Mum so hard to sign me up, although I knew that we were in financial straits. We could not touch the 18,000 Reichsmarks; we would need them for a new start for the family. We always did as if the money was not there and never talked about it. We could not buy anything with our money anyway, not even a chicken. We got food stamps, and went shopping for essentials. These stamps were taken to the store and we had to pay with our money. On the stamps was printed, for example, 100g butter, 1 kg of bread, 200g pork.

Finally, Mum took me from Scherfede to Warburg. We went first by train and then walked on foot from one end of town to the other. Our minister Hirschmeyer, who had come with the same transport from Silesia, had a room at the School Sisters'. We went to see him and Mum explained the situation. The principal then listened to our problem and was willing to accept me for free if I would show the required performance.

The school fee was twenty marks a month and we had to add the costs for the train ticket from initially RM 2.20, later 4.40 daily. That was too much for Mum who only received RM 39 per month for four people. With this money we were supposed to pay RM 9 rent for a nine-square-meter room at Laudage's, which was assigned to us. German families with living space had to accommodate displaced persons by law. We were very fortunate with the family and out of kindness they did not take our money. We had breakfast and dinner in our little room. Thanks to Mum's labour performance, we had a hot lunch at the table of the house owner. My train arrived at 2.40pm in Scherfede and I still had to walk to Rimbeck, where I found my meal in Laudage's kitchen. Mum and Ursula shared a Westphalian bed; I had an iron bed on the other side of the table, where I also did my homework. There was only room for one chair, we children sat on the beds. An army locker and an iron stove completed the sparse furnishings. The locker was sufficient, since we had almost nothing to hang in it anyway. There were no proper mattresses, instead we had straw bags on slats.

As already mentioned, there were only food stamps, since money alone had no value until the currency reform of 1948. The food stamps, however, had an almost inestimable value. One day,

Mum, Ursula, and myself were queuing up in front of the butcher shop before business hours, when we heard the grandmother calling, 'Erich, open the shop, the Polacks are already there!' We were Germans and were now disparagingly referred to as Poles. I was confused. Was it our fault that we had been driven from our homeland?

After six months of employment, Ruth left that butcher and found work at a company by the name of Eschke, a ceramic workshop. Mr. Laudage had the carpenter Gieseler make a bed for her and put it into Elisabeth's room.

Liesel Jüttner, who was found seriously injured under a pile of corpses in February the year before, had also been on our transport to the west. She then worked for a while, married Richard Baumert and had two daughters and a son with him. She was admitted to a nursing home after a few years. The physical and psychological damage of the war was just too big for her and it was impossible to forget the past.

After the currency reform, when there were no more food stamps, all refugees and displaced persons went to the butchers in Scherfede. We now had food again regularly. If you never went hungry, you cannot imagine the feeling of what that meant to us. Everyday Mum milked Laudage's cow and got a liter of milk and two eggs for it. Ursula and I got an egg each for our school sandwiches.

Finally I could go back to school! I loved this school. The first day I went with Zita Fischer, who I already knew, to class 1a, which consisted only of Catholic girl students whereas class 1b consisted of Catholic and Protestant girl students. I was the 42nd student and had to sit in the back row. It was a solid bench and I did not feel particularly comfortable in the beginning. I was under pressure, my performance had to be good and the further back you sit, the harder it is to concentrate. I looked after my classmates. Marietta and the two Köring girls were in my class being the same age as me; Zita and Ingrid were a year younger.

We all took the train from Scherfede station to Warburg and in Warburg we had to cross some streets together. All in all, the walk was quite long, because the school was located at the opposite end of town. We needed half an hour, plus a steep ascent shortly before the school. Poor Marietta had asthma and we often helped her up the hill.

My first assignment in science class was to describe different types of cabbage. Brussels sprouts and kale I did not know until we arrived in Rimbeck. Brussels sprouts was one of the more noble vegetables for Sundays. Kale I knew only as mud from the cans of the cannery in Parchwitz, which was cooked with pork fat and sausage. Not a remarkable meal....

At this point I would like to send a thank you to the American Quakers, who donated a daily school meal for the German children. Ursula and I got meals from 1947 onwards. It was alternately pea soup and porridge, on Wednesdays there was a thick peanut butter roll. Sometimes we had raisins in milk soup, but I loved the peanut butter rolls! Vulnerable children such as refugees, did not need to pay anything, all the others paid a small amount weekly. I collected the money for a while, kept the record book and handed both to the teacher. That was quite a responsible job and I felt a bit more accepted and respected. After the long years of fear and the feeling of subjection I had a first glimpse of a decent life again. I had to hold on and make no mistake. Farmers' children were, of course, exempt from these school lunches, they brought their own food from home instead. They were also the strongest and loudest among the students. Sometimes I was jealous, and then I needed to be alone. Again and again I remembered my father and I often wanted to share my food with him, so he would not starve to death in Siberia. I often prayed for him quietly on the train and clearly saw his face right before me. He smiled with his eyes, his mouth moved a little. I would have given anything to lie back in his strong arms. I wanted to go with him to the horses or just sit in the back seat of our car and drive to wherever. Maybe that would never happen again, the prospects were very poor. My heart was pounding and I felt helpless, alone.

The milk soup was made with milk powder and was surely extended with more water than anticipated. Sometimes it was thick and had flour lumps in it. The soups were cooked by the Sisters in the kitchen, where they also made the bread and then distributed food in the big break in the schoolyard. We had to bring bowls and spoons from home and take them back daily. The school also had a boarding school and the girls who lived far away only went home on holidays. I was grateful that I did not have to live at the boarding school. That way I could at least see my Mum and sisters every day and was not alone.

Good train connections were scarce and the trip expensive. On special occasions we finished school after only four hours, and then we had to manage to catch a long-distance train, which was always crowded with people and their backpacks, but somehow we always found seats. The townspeople tried to exchange their saved belongings for food in the countryside. I remember a sermon where the pastor was going strongly against the hardness of heart and asked if the farmers would now dress the cowsheds with carpets.

In the early postwar years, potatoes were a staple diet. Mum and Mrs. Laudage went every day into the garden, which was not directly located at the house, to plant and harvest there. Every bit of the garden was used for growing vegetables and we had a little variety to the potatoes. There was also lettuce and beans; the beans were called pig beans in Silesia and were not eaten by humans there. In the morning we would put pieces of bread into a bowl and pour a little hot milk over it, sometimes we had a small amount of sugar with it. Mum made scrambled eggs mixed with flour for our lunches. The Dittrich's and the other families complained about the rudeness of their landlords, who made it hard for them fetching water or they did not give them enough space in the basement. There were no real jobs. In spring and summer of 1947 the younger women went to replant the woods, where they were taken by British military vehicles.

Work was popular, although it was very poorly paid. Mum tried to get a piece of land for growing vegetables, and it was then promised her. In return she had to help with the harvest and wash the dishes at parties. She found work at an inn where the owner also had some land. The following year she was given a patch of land that needed to be cultured from scratch. The owner's name was also Laudage, but he was not related to our landlord. The small piece of land was poor and located outside the so-called White Wood in the forest, where there was not even water for the plants. Mum had to turn the soil, plant potatoes and see if anything came of it. I do not know where she got the seeds from, but I suppose that they came from the blacksmith Laudage. With the food stamps we got bread and small amounts of fat, everything was still rationed.

During the holidays, Elisabeth showed me what was going on in Rimbeck: her friends Hilde Schäfers, Elisabeth Peine, the White Wood in the north and the Black Wood in the south of Rimbeck. At the White Wood there was a huge ancient grave and the spring of the Nauer Creek. There we went swimming in the freezing cold water, which of course was not any warmer in a hot summer. From then on it was four of us on Sundays. Elisabeth Peine was the only child of a railway official. Hilde was a farmer's daughter, the eldest of four children; later another little sister was born, when Hilde was sixteen. She had to help a lot at home and her father was very generous to us refugees. He did not clean up the fields like the other farmers so that we could pick up vegetables. In the summer we harvested together. Mum took us to help, but when it went toward eleven o'clock, I blacked out regularly and had to sit in the shade. The community's threshing machine threshed what Mum and the others had collected. We then went to the mill and exchanged everything for flour.

The winter came and I had neither shoes nor a coat. From a collection bin I got an old, worn gray coat and I do not know how to describe it. Calling such a rag a coat was an insult to all proper coats. Only the longitudinal fibers were still intact at the pockets, the transverse threads were completely worn out. It was not a real winter coat, for it was way too thin, I cannot even say whether it ever had some sort of lining before. So I wore it and was still freezing, but I had nothing else.

I had a pair of rubber overshoes from my grandmother which Mum had carried in her bag when we left Heidau. Bernhard Laudage fitted small blocks of wood from his workplace into the heels, since I had no shoes to wear inside. The overshoes were too big for me, so they had to be stuffed with newspaper. I put the overshoes on with only socks inside and went to school. My feet were never warm in these things, so I took them off during class, which helped a little. It was not customary for us to be called to the blackboard, so I got away with it. Until the next break my feet were warm, and of course during the break they got cold and the whole process started all over again. I could not walk properly and had to carefully lift my feet not to destroy the thin soles. How I envied some children for their proper winter clothing!

Vicar Weber organized a Christmas party with the Catholic youth and all the children of refugees were given a small gift. Mine consisted of a pair of white, hand-knitted gloves made of cotton. Poems were recited that evening and my poem was 'Der Halligmatrose' and it goes like this:

Kaptain, ich bitt´ euch, lasst mich fort,
O lasset mich frei, sonst lauf ich von Bord,
Ich muss heim, muss heim nach der Hallig!
Schon sind vergangen drei ganze Jahr,
Dass ich stets zu Schiff, dass ich dort nicht war,
Auf der Hallig, der lieben Hallig.

Nein, Jasper, nein, das sag´ ich dir,
Noch diese Reise machst du mit mir,
Dann darfst du gehn nach der Hallig.

Doch sage mir, Jasper, was willst du dort?
Es ist ein so öder, armseliger Ort,
Die kleine, einsame Hallig.

Ach, mein Kapitän, dort ist's wohl gut,
Und an keinem Ort wird mir so zumut,
So wohl als auf der Hallig;
Und mein Weib hat um mich manch traurige Nacht,
Hab' so lang nicht gesehn, wie mein Kind mir gelacht
Und Haus und Hof auf der Hallig.

So höre denn, Jasper, was ich dir sag':
Es ist gekommen ein böser Tag,
Ein böser Tag für die Hallig;
Auch die Schafe und Lämmer sind fortgespült,
Auch dein Haus ist fort, deine Wurt zerwühlt;
Was wolltest du tun auf der Hallig?

Doch sollst du nicht hin, vorbei ist die Not,
Dein Weib ist tot, und dein Kind ist tot,
Ertrunken beid' auf der Hallig.
Auch die Schafe und Lämmer sind fortgespült,
Auch dein Haus ist fort, deine Wurt zerwühlt;
Was wolltest du tun auf der Hallig?

Ach Gott, Kapitän, ist das geschehn!
Alles soll ich nicht wiedersehn,
Was lieb mir war auf der Hallig?
Und ihr fragt mich noch, was ich dort will tun?
Will sterben und im Grase ruhn
Auf der Hallig, der lieben Hallig.

Hermann Allmers, 1821-1902

The Sailor from the Island

Captain, I beg you, let me go,
O let me go, otherwise I'll run off the boat,
I must go home, must go home to the island!
Already three whole years have passed,
I've always been aboard, never back there,
On the island, the beloved island.

No, Jasper no, I'm telling you,
Even do this trip for me,
Then you can go to the island.
But tell me, Jasper, what will you do there?
It is such a dreary, miserable place,
The small, solitary island.

Oh, my Captain, there's a good place for me
And no place I like so much,
So well as on the island;
And my wife has spent some sad nights,
Have not seen my child laughing in a long time
And my house and land on the island.

Listen, then, Jasper, what I'm telling you:
It's been a bad day
A bad day for the island;
Even the sheep and lambs are washed away,
Also, your house is gone, so is your land;
What did you want to do on the island?
But you should not go there, the damage is done,
Your wife is dead, and thy child is dead,
Drowned both on the island.
Even the sheep and lambs are washed away,
Also, your house is gone, so is your land;
What did you want to do on the island?

Oh God, Captain, has this happened?

Nothing I shall see again,
What I liked on the island?
And yet you ask me what I want to do there?
Want to die and rest in the grass;
On the island, the beloved island.

When I think about it now I cannot understand why would you give such a poem to a child that just had survived the war? What were they thinking?

The vicar tried hard to integrate the refugees. We were probably the only Catholics and so benefited the most. He gave me extra tuition in the fall so I could go to Holy Communion. On that special day a classmate gave me a bowl of fresh fruits and Mrs. Laudage made a cake that we all enjoyed. I had a glass of milk, too, and I felt a bit more accepted. I was happy. The celebrations in Rimbeck were mainly ecclesiastical. On Christmas Day of 1946 the celebration took place at the Laudage Inn where the boys' music group played their instruments. They were fourteen to eighteen years old and played guitar, mandolin and drums and had been taught by the vicar.

There was no Christmas tree in the Laudage house, for there was no room for it. The living room, where Mr. Laudage had his desk was not heated, since there was no fuel. The only warm place was in the kitchen because the stove was fired with wood, we could not heat the living room as well. There was only a small wreath of fir twigs with a candle in the middle. For us it was the second Christmas in a row without Dad. The Laudage family had lost their son that year and so we celebrated quietly. It was another cold winter night.

A package from Saxony arrived. Ursula and Marianne Köhler who had been alternately employed in Heidau by Dad did send us presents. Mum gave me a photo album. Much later I got photos every now and then to put in. Cameras were very rare and even if someone had one did not necessarily have a film for it. I certainly had neither and so for many years there were no pictures taken. I still have that album to this day.

Birthdays were not celebrated in Rimbeck, only name-days. Except for me there was no one named Ingeborg and only my two middle names were listed on the calendar of the saints, but they did not count. Today Ingeborg is listed on July 30th. The Holy Ingeborg was a Swedish princess who married a French king. Had I only known this back then!

Economically, we remained very poor. All the money we earned was just enough for food and we were not able to save anything. The townspeople were still coming to the villages and exchanged just about anything for food. They were in a really bad situation. Mrs. Laudage never took anything from them. Whoever wanted something to eat got a bowl of soup from the big pot as long as the supply was sufficient. In case there was not enough left for us in the evening it was stretched with hot water and we had a slice of bread with it. There was another family in Rimbeck that gave a lot and took nothing in return. The housewife and mother died of tuberculosis; two children had contracted the same severe disease. They gave too much, everything. Not too long after they died as well. During this hardship you could learn a lot about living together and people in general. Those, who had very little shared a lot, more than anyone else.

Once, while she was working in the fields, Mum talked about her former home back in Heidau and thus earned only scorn and ridicule, when she was being asked how many horses they have had there. She vowed then never to talk about home again. It happened to me as well, because I said that I used to have both roller skates *and* ice skates. I never spoke about our lost property at school anymore. There was a cruel saying:

"They came from the east
Live at our expense.
They each had 1,000 acres of land
and they never met Hitler."

That was mean and wrong, and we never got the opportunity to present our side of the story. We never heard a bad word coming from the Laudage family. They all treated Mum with respect and us kids like their own. At this time Mr. Laudage was our surrogate father and his wife mother to us all. I think that is something that has always distinguished the Maiwald family: Never give up, adapt to the conditions and stick together as a family. We only had a chance to survive because we swallowed our pride, even if it was bitter.

Ursula also found a new friend. Her classmate Elsmarie had moved with her mother and sister from the city to her grandparents who operated a bakery in Rimbeck. They had been 'bombed' in the city, a word that is forgotten today. The West Germans were preferred by the government and we were still second class people. One of my new friends asked for a new pair of shoes and received what she wanted although she still had another pair at home. I did not even get one pair.

I have to thank Elisabeth for my integration in Rimbeck. She took me to the Catholic Youth Choir, which also had a theater group. There was one performance a year, and once I even got the lead role as Donna Columbina, which I enjoyed very much. We were dressed in borrowed costumes from a theater wardrobe and my dress fitted perfectly after minor alterations. I had never had such a beautiful dress before. When I was seventeen years old I went with Marietta and joined the Scherfede Sports Club.

-16-

Bread and Blood

After a terrible and exhausting transport my father arrived in Russia, in Chelyabinsk, Magnitogorsk in the Urals, to be precise. At first he had to work there as a lumberjack, then in a lead mine. The accommodation was primitive and inadequate without hygiene whatsoever. The food consisted of stale bread and water and perhaps an egg on Sunday. The camps were overcrowded; death was a constant companion.

There is a request, still in existence today, which is addressed to the Red Cross, Central Tracing Department for prisoners of war and civilian internees from my father with the date October 31st, 1946. The sender's details were: Artur Maiwald, CCCP-Moscow, Red Cross P.O. Box 10227. It was the first time in eighteen months after his capture in Heidau that he was allowed to ask about us. Mum had also turned to the Red Cross from Rimbeck and to the agreed address of Mr. Schulze in Leipzig. She mailed the first card to Mr. Schulze, who immediately answered with a letter. We knew no one with a telephone and everything went very slowly. The joy was indescribable: Dad was alive! His first card was dated January 16th, 1947 saying that he had received the Christmas cards from us, we should not worry and he would be home soon.

Artur's card

We saw Uncle Otto in 1947 in Rimbeck again when he was on his way to Wilhemshaven, where he was offered a job as head of a tannery. He stayed in a room with Franz and Bernhard. Shortly before his departure, he forgot his briefcase next to a chair. By the time we found it, it was too late. A few days later a letter arrived from Otto and he wrote that he would like to have is bag forwarded. Mum mailed the content, but not the bag itself, which then became my school bag. It was made of brown, quite worn leather and had a broken buckle. For me however, it was a welcome improvement, because until then I had only a cardboard folder for my books, which fell apart gradually.

In the summer of the same year Uncle Otto posted black leather and I got my first pair of shoes made in a long time. Mum and I went ten kilometers on foot to the town of Wormeln, on the other side of Warburg. A shoemaker from Heidau made me a pair of shoes that did not look very sporty, but they were strong and durable. Unfortunately, the leather was not enough for a pair of winter boots.

On Christmas Eve 1947 a whole group of young people including me walked from Rimbeck to Midnight Mass to the town of Kleinenberg and returned home after midnight. Elisabeth and her brothers were also there, and so I was allowed to go, too. It was a starry winter night, which I remember very well. Everything was peaceful and no one needed to be afraid. Although we now had lived in Rimbeck for a year and a half, the memory of the war was still very fresh and that is why I can remember this quiet night. On that long walk in the snow I had to think of the many dead I had seen on the main road in Heidau. They did not have the luck we had. Again we had a Christmas without our father.

On public holidays, Mrs. Laudage always made a special effort with lunch. Then it was not the time for just any food or leftovers. Sometimes there was a slice of ham fried like a steak, potato and gravy, and mostly homemade sauerkraut.

On Sundays during the winter evenings we gathered in the church and played games. There were no other rooms available for the youth and since Elisabeth, her brothers and friends were also there, we had lots of fun.

We received more cards from Dad dated August 18th, October 15th and December 12th. All of them were very short. The card dated January 5th, 1948 (Mum's birthday) was for the first time more detailed. He wrote all encrypted about coming home and that he wanted to work in his profession again. He also wanted to contact Mr. Schulze and bring everything back into motion again as it had been before the war. Schulze had had sought him a tannery in the town of Lospuden at the time, but because of the war events Dad never got to it. Mum should look after the money and if necessary, purchase a small business or farm near Leipzig before the Reichsmarks dropped any further. Mum had written to him beforehand, also encrypted, that she still had Reichsmarks left. Dad did not know that it was absolutely impossible to buy anything. We had cash, but there was nothing to buy. Absolutely everything was rationed and could only be bought in conjunction with ration coupons. Mum would certainly have bought a goat, but there was not even a chicken available. The Laudage's did not know about our money at the beginning. Later on they did and they advised Mum to go to a bank in the village of Marsberg, so the Rimbeck bankers would not know anything about it. Such an amount would have created quite a stir in the village. The Laudage's understood the situation we were in and there was never a jealous word. We were very lucky.

On February 14th, 1948 Dad congratulated me to my 14th birthday and wrote that he would be home to celebrate Ruth's 19th birthday. He also wrote for the first time that he was sick and felt more like a guest at the hospital. In captivity he was hungry every single day, plus the neverending months of winter...

Dad suffered his second stroke and spent many weeks in hospital where he was supposed to recover. The German physician and co-prisoner Dr. Hellhacke from the city of Iserlohn got him in there and looked after him. Dad also wrote about his future plans and that we should not worry too much, and that he would run the show very soon. On March 13th he wrote that he was feeling better at a rest home and he weighed 65 kgs again.

One transport had already left for Germany; two more would follow, where he hoped to be on either of them. More cards followed on April 7th, June 9th, July 10th, and August 23rd, where he told us to keep our courage and stay put, he would come home and everything will be all right again. He had gained more weight and was now at about 70 kgs.

The Marshall Plan was announced, but due to the bad currency situation could not be put into action at first. A currency reform should have been held after the war, but the Allied Control Council could not agree and it took until 1948. There was a four-power administration in Germany and after the failure of negotiations, the western powers without the Soviet Union prepared a reform in the three zones of occupation. The new money had already been printed in the USA in October 1947 and was introduced on June 20th, 1948. We had heard about it two days earlier at the butcher shop as a customer said she had heard it on the radio. The radio stations were operated by the military, in our case by the British power.

Germans were only allowed to exchange 40, - Deutsche Mark 'bounty' (per head) for old Reichsmarks, while at the same token wages, salaries and rents were re-evaluated 1:1. Savings accounts were re-evaluated 1:10. Since we had no land and no values, we were among the big losers. Our cash dropped overnight from 18,000 to 1,800, which we did not know at the time. We had practically lost everything. Ludwig Erhard, then Minister of Economics, abolished the price-fixing and production controls that had been enacted by the military administration. This exceeded his authority, but he succeeded with this courageous step. He said, 'The only coupon now is the Deutsche Mark.'

18,000 was the price of a small farm we could not buy...

We were amazed when we saw the windows in Warburg filled with some of previously hoarded goods. There was so much clothing that had not been available during or shortly after the war. We could not believe it! How many people could have been saved? All the things had been hidden away and we almost froze to death. I was devastated, to say the least.

The black market disappeared in silence, while everything was much more expensive and unemployment went up dramatically.

In the eastern Soviet occupation zone, where my friend Gisel and her family lived, the currency reform took place on June 23rd, 1948. There was no new money printed, instead the old Reichsmark banknotes had coupons attached. Each citizen was given 70 marks. The standard of living did not improve since the rationing was retained. So we had two different systems in a single country. What would be next?

(A summary of the currency reform is to be found at the end of this book)

-17-

The Family and the Carrot

On Sunday evening October 3rd, 1948, Mum, Ursula and I were sitting on the edges of the beds in our little room. Elisabeth's brother Bernhard came to ask me out for a dance in November. Of course, he needed Mum's permission first. Elisabeth would come too and minors accompanied by adults were allowed to stay until 10pm. It was St. Elisabeth Day, a village festival on November 19th. I was fourteen and a half and Mum gave her consent. 'Until then, you have enough time to practice,' he said, laughing. Of course, this invitation was an honour for me. I had already noticed that he had occupied the laundry room every morning for the last few weeks when I wanted to do my morning toilet. Then he would leave generously and make room for me. There was no bathroom in the house, and the laundry room with its brick basin was used for everything that had to do with water. Even the buckets for the animals were filled there. On Saturdays the big boiler was filled with water and heated. Then we took the zinc tub off the hook and took our baths in a pre-arranged order.

Dad eventually got a place on a transport home and reached Rimbeck that very evening. He found the Laudage house and heard us laughing inside. He then came closer and had a look through the window. We did not notice him, and he was pleased when he saw us in good spirits.

Dad knocked on the door, Mr. Laudage opened it and asked him inside. After a moment the door was opened to our room and it took our breath away. This was the happiest moment in my life: Dad was back!

He was wearing an old greasy wool jacket, dirty trousers, rags and wooden galoshes on his feet. His face was swollen; he had very short hair and was barely recognizable. When the Russians captured him in Heidau he had been forty, young and strong, and now we saw an old man, sick and ragged at forty-three. However, we were overjoyed to be able to hug him again. This feeling was indescribable, and we never wanted to let go of him again. Everyone had tears in their eyes and my heart was pounding.

He had made it!

Ruth was missing at that time, for she was dancing with her boyfriend Heinz and a few other friends at the station. Bernhard, Elisabeth and myself ran off to fetch her. When we all came back Dad had taken off his jacket, which was burned a few days later together with the foot-bandages. He was sitting on the only chair at the table and had a small meal in front of him. It was late and the bed situation was quickly and easily arranged. Elisabeth and I slept in her bed, Ruth slept in the other one in the same room. The rest of the family shared our little room. In my excitement I could hardly sleep and my only thought was: We are a family again. Now everything will be all right!

On his discharge papers in German and English the following was noted:

Discharge amount: DM 40.00 signed by the Paymaster. Later it was added: 5/10/1948: financial aid DM 25.00.

For clothing DM 170.00 18/12/1948, and DM 190.00, undated.

The whole form had been stamped by the official administration of the Warburg District. Dad also carried papers, which confirmed that he was one hundred percent disabled and was entitled to receive a small pension.

Dad rested from the long and arduous journey. A few days after his arrival, we went through the village and suddenly he saw a carrot lying on the sidewalk. He picked it up, put it in his pocket and said to me softly, 'For later.'

Dad also told me a story of his captivity. To everyone's surprise, one day there was a competition in which the prisoners should participate. The task was the invention and construction of a potato peeler and the winner would be released from the prison camp and sent home. Dad signed up because he liked the challenge and had nothing to lose. In the competition there were some engineers but that did not particularly impress my father. His machine consisted of a drum that was filled with potatoes and sand. You could either use a hand-crank or an electric motor. The potatoes had a relatively loose skin because they were picked too early. The machine worked perfectly and Dad won the competition. The machines of the engineers were too complicated for the Russian judges. Despite his victory our father was not sent home early. Max Schulze wrote to Mum, that Dad should not make himself indispensable.

One day Dad met a fellow prisoner from the town of Bonenburg, Warburg District at the prison camp, and told him that we had found shelter at a blacksmith's home named Laudage. This man knew the Laudage family and told my father that we were living with good people and he needed not to worry. The good deeds of the family had travelled over thousands of kilometers to the Urals! At the worst time my father weighed only forty-six kilograms and had to perform extremely hard labour. Only when the temperatures reached below minus forty degrees Celsius they no longer had to work and stayed at the camp.

Many prisoners died in labour camps and it was almost a miracle that anyone ever came out alive. Of all the prisoners only ten percent came back to Germany. There was very little food, a constant cold, no days off, and no sanitation. The work in the lead mine made everyone ill, many were coughing all day and died painfully. The men were lowered into the pits in open steel cages without any safety precautions and brought back up again after work. Injuries were common, and were only treated poorly. A human life was worth nothing and the prisoners were reminded of it daily. After a few months my father gave up counting the dead bodies. He always said a silent prayer. At the same time he asked for strength for his surviving friends and himself.

The man from Bonenburg did not make it to the transit, and he never saw home and family again. After a short recovery time Dad went to his friend's family and told them about his time in Siberia and that the father and husband had been a fair and decent man. He was proud to have met him and he would treasure the friendly memories. As hardened as Dad now was, during his description he shed a few tears and was not ashamed of them.

Dad always was a very brave man. He got up and focused on his new situation in Rimbeck, took out a small notebook and wrote something down. I never read it, maybe there were new ideas that he wanted to put into action. It probably helped him to persevere and keep going. His first pair of shoes was given to him by the vicar who then had only one pair of shoes for himself. In the photo of his new driver license Dad was wearing donated clothes.

Ruth had left her first workplace and was now working at a ceramic factory in Warburg, where she painted jars and bowls. This job did not last long, because the company by the name of Eschke soon went bankrupt, as well as many other companies. It was a very difficult time, the war had ended three years ago and it seemed that the hard times would continue for some time at the economic level.

The 39 Reichsmarks, which Mum had received for the family, were immediately withdrawn completely when Dad got his pension in November 1948. We never received a present from our country. Mrs. Laudage was sick and Mum helped our hosts whenever she could. The household was not small and they had to look after the animals, the garden, a small field, and the washing without a washing machine. I sometimes cleaned our small room in order to relieve Mum.

Of course there was also a lot of paperwork to be done that had to do with the organization and reconstruction of the state. Dad once had to fill out a questionnaire:

The way of my deportation to the Soviet Union

Transit camp before being transported: Beuthen, Upper Silesia, prison.

Loading station: Freight Station

Exit 16 April 1945, 10am

Number of men in the car: 42

Probable total number: 1,500

Arrival in Kopesk 20 May 1945

Nearest city: Chelyabinsk

Accommodation: wooden barracks

Work: coal shaft kolkhoz

With me came into this camp: 2,000 civilians, 1,000 prisoners of war.

The way I was captured by the collective stock: I was together with two civilians, prisoners of war. Transported by truck in March 1945. Liegnitz in basements from 2 March to 30 March

4,000-5,000 prisoners. Places we passed on my transport: Orel, Lviv, Kiev, Kharkov, Ki ...?

Number of people who died in transit: approx. 500

Persons who were also on my transport:

Altmann, Paul	Ohlau, Silesia dead
Reisner, Bruno	Kotzenau, Silesia dead
Kotz, Paul	Liegnitz, Silesia dead
Rendschmidt ?	Teacher, Liegnitz dead
Konrad ?	Stonemason dead

Anita Pohl from Heidau also survived the labour camp in Siberia, and arrived in Scherfede after Dad and was reunited with her parents. There she met a British man, married and moved with him to England.

At this point I would like to write about a different fate. Upper Silesia had a special status in relation to the expulsion. The Germans living there were given the choice whether to stay or leave their homes and move to the west. There were of course some conditions to obey. One for instance was that it was no longer allowed to speak German and the children had to go to

Polish schools. A family by the name of Montag lived there in a small village and the father Heinrich also had fallen into Russian captivity. The rest of the family, the mother and three children, remained in the village on their farm, because the mother said, 'We have to stay here, how else will your father find us after they discharge him? We will wait for him right here.'

In 1948, Heinrich was sent back to Germany, but Upper Silesia was now part of Poland and was behind the Iron Curtain. In the meantime his wife had died from a disease and the children were living in a Polish orphanage. Heinrich got their address through the Red Cross, but travelling into Poland was very difficult and he was afraid that they might hold him there. The years passed, the oldest daughter married a German man in Poland and the other two children remained in the orphanage because they were too young to work. Finally, in 1959 they were all able to leave and were reunited with their father after fourteen years. The house and farm in Upper Silesia were lost, naturally.

In the winter of 1948 I had a nasty accident. Between classes I slipped on the icy surface in the yard and hit a stone with my head. The school nurse suspected concussion and I was sent home accompanied by a classmate. The nurse wrapped a bandage around my head and I had to stay in bed for two weeks and was not allowed to read. Zita and I swapped our coats because hers had a hood and could therefore mask the bandage. It was the last day at school for me and I was a bit sad that I did not have a proper send off. When I got well again Dad asked me if I wanted to become a doctor. I did not know what to answer and he said, 'You don't need to become a teacher and get annoyed by other people's children.' Only a doctor would have been good enough, and he added, 'We have no money, but we would work very hard to ensure that you can study.'

I did not want everybody working for me since I was not certain if I could go all the way. My certificates had become better and better, I had only 'A's' and 'B's' in all subjects, not one 'C.' It would have been sufficient for an application.

It was cheap to buy land in Scherfede. The area was called "Auf der Walme" and it was about two to three acres in size. Dad looked into it, but it was useless for his purposes.

On one of our walks, I showed Dad the area outside the White Wood, where we had gathered beechnuts. Although he suffered fluid retention in his legs, he was looking for suitable premises to set up a new tannery and he found a former distillery in Rimbeck. There were two cellar rooms in the building he could rent and a carpenter named Mr. Fuest made two vessels for him. Due to his severe disability, he could not be the owner himself, and so Mum, Ruth and I went into a partnership and founded a company called Maiwald KG. We were able to apply for a construction loan and purchased the first machine. At first, our parents worked alone and produced various types of furs. Mum and I picked up sacks with raw skins from the train station in Scherfede using a hand-cart. After a while Dad decided to produce leather, because there was not enough demand for furs. He bought used sewing machines and a sewing room was set up on the first floor of the same building. Soon after, five seamstresses were employed and I became a cutter. I had to quit school which was not easy for me. There went the dream of studying at a university. The vicar lent us his little portable typewriter and Ruth took care of the correspondence. She also did the first accounting. From a company called Deuter, Dad got another pair of shoes after he had contacted them and got some business. Deuter had already been customers in the Heidau times.

Thea was responsible for the cuts, and had gone to a commercial school in the city of Kassel. She was ten years older than me and during the war she used to work at the railway. When the men returned from captivity she quit there voluntarily and her position was then occupied by an unemployed father. She was a great friend and appreciated by all. Thea married at the age of thirty when her fiancé came home late from captivity.

Some time later Dad mentioned that he wanted to introduce a young friend from prison camp to Ruth, because he thought that this man could be his successor. He then put this idea aside when he saw that Ruth was getting engaged to Heinz Scholle, a man from Scherfede. There was still no work for Ruth, she was now twenty-one and could not find new employment after the ceramic painting job.

In late 1948 I got a pair of brown shoes from a shoe shop in Warburg, which I liked a lot. I still had no decent winter coat and had to do something about it. From my pocket money I earned as a cutter I bought a residual fabric in a store called Simon. Thea agreed to make me a coat and we got going. It had capped sleeves, no collar and no lining because the fabric was insufficient. At the same time, Elisabeth also had a coat made by Thea. The fabric was manufactured on Thea's loom and she finished the two projects in no time. Ursula went to school for eight years, and thereafter three years of trade school. She was working five days a week with us at the factory and went one day a week to trade school.

Laudage's had relatives in America and one day they received a parcel from them. From then on Mrs. Laudage made fine wheat flour pudding on Saturdays and let it cool down so we had it cold on Sundays and public holidays. However, I cannot remember having cakes, but I know that Mrs. Laudage always looked forward to the coffee beans she would find in the parcels. She had low blood pressure and relied on the coffee.

Our family left the Laudage household in the spring of 1949 because we were allocated to an apartment with a large kitchen and two small rooms above Schroeder's inn. Mr. Laudage was so nice and gave our parents and Ruth the three beds as a gift. Ursula and I borrowed the bed of the deceased parents of Ida Fuest. She also gave us dining room furniture for DM 100 per year. It was a new beginning for us. In addition Mrs. Laudage gave us an old wardrobe that had no rod for coat hangers but hooks instead. I believe the wardrobe was probably from the 19th century. They also gave us an old but functional stove.

Since we had no bathroom Mum and Dad used a makeshift shower in the basement of the tannery and we children had a bath in a tin tub in our kitchen. The toilet was down the hall and was shared with another tenant. In order to make money we had to change our production. We began to manufacture leather pants and put ads in the newspapers. We made motorcycle clothing from goat leather. Our range covered pants and jackets with reinforced elbows, kidney protection, gloves and hoods. It was all very, very difficult, but we did not give up. Dad's pension was very small, at first it was 80 Deutsche Marks, years later it went up to 120. One day, Dad surprised everyone with a car, which was a pre-war DKW that could not be locked anymore. Dad gave us a few driving lessons, that was totally new to us. At first it was a bit difficult with the gear change, but then it went very well. I did not sign up at the driving school for lack of funds and never wasted a second thought. The license was not a priority and could wait.

Once my father and I were in Paderborn and I had to drive back because he felt so miserable that he could no longer concentrate. He had developed ulcers from the Russian injections and got really sick and asked me to take the wheel. At that time, not many cars were on the road and I only had to overtake one horse-drawn carriage, loaded with wood. Later we had a representative who went bankrupt and could not pay for the goods. He had an old Opel, which had been used in the war. Dad took this Opel instead and replaced the DKW which he sold because it was in better condition and yielded more money. The Opel had torn upholstery and we dressed it up with fabric lining. It was driven at least another year before we were able to buy a pre-owned Opel Rekord.

Business was always up and down again until we got a request for calf skin backpacks from Uruguay, which should be made after the pattern of the former Wehrmacht ones. To make it all happen we needed expensive new machinery, especially a knife sharpening machine. Dad sat down and made the drawings, which he passed on to the locksmith Josef Schulte in Rimbeck. He was a very talented man and built the machine in a short time. Josef had fought in World War I and had lost most of his fellow soldiers at Verdun, France. His daughter Klothilde died in 1945 at the young age of eighteen because of a congenital heart valve defect, which you can operate these days. Besides her, he and his wife Maria had four sons. The family had to leave their home right before Easter 1945 and flee to the Rimbeck forest, because American troops had occupied the houses and no one wanted to become a target. When they returned after two days, the house had numerous bullet holes and was deserted. The US troops had moved east. The Schulte brothers were too young for the military and thus were spared.

On Christmas Day 1949 I got new pajamas which were powder blue with little flowers and I was very happy and thankful. It was a forgotten piece of clothing since I had not had one in almost five years, but I got used to it. That was another small step back to normality.

The tannery in Rimbeck

In 1950 I was sixteen and Mum shared the money she earned from a little side job with Ruth and me. She tanned rabbit furs or even dear skins for neighbours and the park ranger. That was our only income for years. With that money we bought our clothes, which means we had to save a long time before we could buy the fabric. Sometimes I would then make myself a skirt during sewing lessons at the Catholic Sister's house. Once I even made my first pair of trousers out of worn men's trousers. Originally the trousers had been given to Dad, but they were too short and too wide. The lining of our motorcycle hoods, gloves and jackets were bought at the department store Simon in Scherfede.

I had nothing in my wallet when I needed money for a flower bouquet for my friend Bernhard, who was in hospital to have his appendix removed. He had asked for some snowdrops from the garden. I could not find any and I did not know what to do other than taking eighty Pfennige (cents) from the old box that served as the company's register. Then I went to the Ortwein nursery and bought a bunch of primroses and took them to Bernhard. This incident bothered me for a long time until I was able to return the money.

In the summer of 1950 we came to a point when we had to find new clients. There were still batches of leather clothes in stock when we ran out of customers. The summer holidays began and I sat down with Thea, thinking how we might boost sales. We wanted to reach out to more villages and go from house to house, submit samples and save the business. Dad said to us, 'Bear in mind that you might need to have a business license.'

I asked the local policeman Mr. Hohenstein and he said if we wanted to try just once, we would certainly not be charged, but we should not just rely on him. Anyway, Dad drove us to the village of Wethen and we marched off. We went through all the streets and alleys, but since it was only a small place we soon had come to an end with only average success. The village of Rhoden was next, where we expected more orders. We also went door to door there and showed our samples around. It worked quite well, and around four o'clock in the afternoon our order book was full. From Rhoden we walked home after we had eaten our sandwiches at the roadside. We had actually planned a bike ride before on this very day, but unfortunately Thea, two seamstresses and I had no bicycles and the youth hostels were still closed. We did not know how to organize accommodation since everyone of us had contacted relatives and acquaintances, but to no avail. We had very little money and so we could not afford a vacation. Instead, the two Elisabeth's, Hilde and I rode our bicycles on Sunday to Lake Diemel which was not too far. I was able to borrow a bicycle and we took off after morning Mass. We had a nice day! We went for a swim, ate our sandwiches and talked about various things. On the way home we had bad luck with Elisabeth's bicycle. Suddenly the rear tire lost air and we had to stop. We still had the city of Wrexen ahead of us and time was running out. At that point we had about seven kilometers to go and Elisabeth had to get back to evening prayer! We could not repair the tube and had to come up very quickly with a plan. We ended up taking turns and pushed the damaged bike, and each of us ran as fast as the others rode their bikes. We arrived on time and no one noticed any of this.

In November 1950 we went to friends who had a larger kitchen and learned to dance there. A couple of young people from the village showed us the steps and I think we did quite well. There were only a few who could go to dance classes. We certainly had no money for such extravagances. There was an old record player in the house and we played the records that had survived the war.

In 1952, Dad bought ten packs of razor blades from a travelling salesman who threw in a wristwatch to sweeten the deal. Dad chose a ladies' watch and gave it to me. I was flattered! I had my very first watch at the age of eighteen, and when I was reading the time sometimes the memory of Heidau came back, when the Russian soldiers shouted, 'Uri, Uri!' and threatened us.

The DKW car

Dad's brother Otto came for a visit to Rimbeck. He stayed for about a week and had long conversations with Dad. For seven years they had not seen each other; now they were both very ill and still had to work hard. When the time of parting came, they looked serious and embraced one another. Maybe they already knew then, that it would be for the last time ever. Some time later, Dad took the train to attend Otto's funeral.

During this period a letter from Krause's daughter Grete reached Mum. She had gotten our address thanks to the Red Cross and asked what had become of her father Hans. Mum replied with a letter the next day and she never mentioned his real character and the crimes he had committed...

We had the most primitive tannery in the world. It was powered by a coal fire and a motor with transmission, where the belts had to be shifted from wheel to wheel to put the machinery into motion. Heaven knows how hard our parents had to work and that had terrible consequences. Dad suffered a third stroke and could no longer work the calf skins. The doctor came and advised bed rest for several weeks. There were no infusions or medications, as they are common today and Dad had to suffer a lot. I was working with a heavy pair of scissors in the cutting room. It severely damaged my finger bones, which could never be repaired. Even today I can still feel the imprints of those scissors.

We were looking for a specialist and found the son of a tanner from the city of Horn by the name of Karl Stecker to take over Dad's work. Karl helped us for about two weeks, so we could finish the job. Dad told me to ask the locksmith's son Kaspar, called Kapa, if he would help us from now on. Kapa had just finished his second apprenticeship. The first one was landscaping and he had already worked in Lippstadt for a year, but the money was bad. As the third son, he did an apprenticeship at his father's, which took only two instead of three years because he had already completed an apprenticeship. Kapa said yes and from then on he worked with us. It was the year of 1953 and we were already an item for a year.

We had met at the village youth group and became good friends. Sometimes we organized trips together, which would cost next to nothing for hardly anyone had money. Bernhard Laudage had to move to the city and only returned for the weekend to Rimbeck. Kapa and I became very close and I had to make a decision. He was a very slender, dark-haired young man, two years older than me, in short: good-looking with honest eyes. Over the next few months I knew him so well and it was clear to me that I had made the right choice. He was determined, but also reliable and funny and we tried to spend much time together. Because of his work in the tannery, we saw each other every day and maybe my work became a bit more pleasant.

Dad received a financial aid budget, which was determined by marital status and specified property. The sum we are talking about here was 300-900 Deutsche Marks. We got the maximum sum, because we had lost a big house. All data had to be witnessed by someone other than a relative. This amount was not paid at once, but in installments. As the first money arrived our parents did not know if and when the next payment would come. It is true that I could have gone to university with that money. But for me it was too late. I decided that it was better to try coping with life at hand.

In the summer of 1954, the German Football Team won the World Cup with a victory over Hungary. That was so important for our country, because for the first time after so many years and bad memories, Germany was something to count on in the world and the Germans were proud of their team.

With Dad's high blood pressure, heart damage and blindness of his right eye, he was quite restricted. After a phone call Dad and Kapa took the car trying to find an appropriate location for a new tannery. There were a few ads in the journal, "Wild und Hund," which Dad always liked to read.

In Marburg there were buildings for sale, but they did not have adequate water supply. In Friedrichsdorf there was a nice building on a large lot, but the price was way too high and could not be negotiated. Finally, they were lucky: in Friedberg, Hessen, they found a property with an adjacent river and a couple of old buildings and a barn. The price was astronomical for us girls and we discussed the purchase together with Mum and voted against it. Dad had an all-or-nothing attitude, and he replied to our concerns,

'What have we got to lose? We have no down-payment and we don't get a loan from the bank. But we have the opportunity to pay off DM 3,000 annually. That must be possible!'

Dad contacted the attorney Mr. Paetow in the city of Giessen, who represented the sellers. They consisted of five nieces and nephews of the deceased Mr. Seligmann, and lived in America and in Switzerland. So it took a few weeks until they all agreed and we had a new address on May 1st, 1955, exactly 30 years after Dad registered his first tannery.

Still in Rimbeck times there was an opportunity to immigrate to Canada, but Dad would have lost his pension we were all living on. We brought no capital from Rimbeck. We had saved DM 2,000, but that had been used up for the move. Two trucks were loaded with all our belongings which consisted of two tanning vessels, two big drums, a Turner fleshing machine, a circular knife sharpener, a couple of our smaller machines, and our rickety furniture.

The condition of the buildings in Friedberg was far worse than those in Heidau. The buildings were about a hundred and fifty years old and looked more like a castle ruin. Ursula and I slept in the former chemical storage room and woke up every morning with an acrid taste in the mouth and coarse throat. We had no bathroom yet, just a tap of cold water outside the house. Dad found a big old mirror with a partly exfoliated layer of silver which was mounted over the water tap and completed our washing place. There was a primitive toilet on the other side of the yard in one of the workshop rooms. We did not have a proper floor in the house, but only hard-packed earth. It was more of an old barn than a house. The previous owner had used the building only as a factory and warehouse. We had to start all over once again. First, the machines were installed and connected to the mains. The entire electrical system had to be replaced and pipes had to be relocated, which was a lot of hard work. Then we commenced rebuilding the house and after many weeks it was reasonably habitable. Still primitive, but we were able to heat it since the next winter was approaching. We all worked as long as we had daylight and after dinner we went straight to bed. After we moved to Friedberg, my parents, Kapa and I visited Christine and Robert Arlt several times in Frankfurt. They were also invited to our wedding on April 22nd, 1956 and they gave us twelve tea towels and a beautiful bouquet of white lilacs with twenty Deutsche Marks attached.

Wedding in Friedberg: Maria, Josef, Ingeborg, Kapa, Klara and Artur (in front of the tannery)

Later in June we received sad news: my second grandmother Muttel had died. She had lived with one of her sons in a town near Dresden in the German Democratic Republic. My parents, Cousin Ruth and I decided to attend the funeral and take the car. When we arrived at the German-German border, there was a big disappointment: we had no permission to enter by car. The border guards made no exception, and so we discussed what to do. Dad was not well and he suggested that he would rather go home than take the train. I offered to go back with him, but Mum decided otherwise. She climbed back into the car, gave me some money and said, 'You both go ahead and take the train. You are young and you will find your way. This will be the best.' We said goodbye and we girls went back to the border officers. There was a thorough check, and then we entered the German Democratic

Republic. We walked to the station, bought tickets and went to Dresden after a longer waiting period. The carriage was pretty old and the trip was slow. Finally, at half past eleven at night we arrived and did not know where to go. We were hungry and had no accommodation for the night, which seemed so familiar to us both. Then I remembered the address in Dresden, where we still had relatives. The address was Hohe Strasse 123, but we did not know where that was. We were lucky. A railway worker gave us the information we were after and showed us to the last tram that would travel to Hohe Strasse. We quickly ran to the tram stop, because we just saw it arriving. The trip did not take too long and we found the address. In one of the windows the light was still on, whereas the rest of the street was dark. I rang the doorbell and within seconds the door opened. 'What took you so long? We have been waiting for hours to see you,' said the aunt and showed us into the house. Somewhat surprised I looked at Ruth and asked the aunt straight away why she was expecting us. She replied that she and her family had not specifically been waiting for us, but for Muttel's relatives in general. We told them everything from the journey and why we were so late. A simple dinner was prepared for us and we went to bed soon after we had washed ourselves with hot water in a bathtub. Because I was older I had the privilege to go in first, then Ruth. On the next day, we attacked the second part of the journey by travelling with a steamship on the Elbe River. That way we later reached the town of Reichenbach and together we went to the cemetery. I had seen Muttel for the last time in late January 1945 and it felt like yesterday. The casket was closed and so she remains in my memory the way she looked eleven years before. We had been only a few hundred kilometers apart and yet it was a different world. I was in pain and for a short time I did not notice anything around me at all.

The same day, Ruth and I had to report to an officer in the city of Meissen and fill out a form. Our stay was recorded with painstaking accuracy and our travel documents were checked again. We endured it all and I felt deeply sorry that my parents had not come along. A day later we went back home.

-18-

The Farewell

The arduous work determined the whole daily routine and we took no vacations. We only took Sundays and public holidays off, anything else would have been considered lazy among the family. Everybody was very happy when in January 1957 our daughter Andrea was born. Mum and I took turns in taking care of her and we were glad that she was healthy and uncomplicated.

Dad suffered another stroke in 1958, from which he was able to recover again. Fortunately, he could still speak as usual, move around well and even walking gave him no visible problems. Several times before he had gone to Friedberg Hospital due to cardiovascular problems and always had been released. In January 1959 the situation worsened, however, and Ruth, who was pregnant, came to Friedberg and visited Dad at the hospital. She was sitting alone with him as he offered her his full plate and whispered, 'Take it, I'm not hungry.' Apparently he believed that he was still imprisoned in Russia and shortly thereafter could not be addressed. The next day we all went back to him and he held Kapa firmly at his side. He said softly, 'Kapa, get the car and take me home.'

Mum then talked to the physician in charge, who rejected a transport because Daddy was being treated with morphine for the pain. Kapa talked again with our father, and explained the situation. Dad assured him that he wanted no more morphine and that he was ready to leave the hospital. As Kapa saw how important it was to him, he went to get the car which was now a pre-owned, gray Mercedes 180 with the license plate FB-L 1. Dad was taken back home and finally he decided to consult a heart specialist by the name of Professor Pierach in the town of Bad

Nauheim. Due to the urgency a quick appointment was made on Ash Wednesday. Mum told us about Dad's frightening nightmares. When he was awake he saw wild animals in front of him, who gathered around his bed threatening him. He called for an ax and Mum fetched one from the workshop. Of course she was very scared and put it on the floor beside the bed.

The next night I spent in an armchair we had found on the property. With the door open, I was sitting in the adjoining office watching over the sleep of my parents. I did not get tired, because the adrenaline was doing its job and kept me awake.

In 1956 we had bought a black and white TV set that was sitting on Ida's cabinet in front of the bed. On Shrove Tuesday we watched the news together as usual and the subsequent show until around 9:30pm. Then we retired for the night, I sat back in my armchair again.

Ash Wednesday came, the eleventh of February. Dad was terribly cold. He got up and sat on the old sofa, which perhaps had belonged to the previous owner Seligmann. We had found it in the house when we moved in, and it seemed ancient to me. With the help of the heater we poured hot water into a large bowl and he took a long foot bath until he was fairly warm again. At the same time we called our family physician Dr. Stamm. Dad was now so bad, that it was impossible to keep the appointment with Professor Pierach. Dr. Stamm finished his consultations and came to our house. He took a look at Dad and then pulled Mum away. Shortly thereafter, a nurse came from the Friedberg Sister's Home, whose name I do not remember anymore. She gave Dad a sedative and asked Mum to inform the pastor. She had noticed blue spots on his skin and knew what they meant. It was not long before the pastor arrived, who was astonished, because Dad looked quite reasonable again. Calmly he gave him the anointing of the sick.

Mum stayed at Dad's bed and I started to prepare dinner. She came running at half past seven, and called all of us. Dad wanted to sit up in bed. We helped him to put his feet on the floor and propped his back with pillows. He did not say a word, and I looked into his face. Within a second, I saw the most important things and events we shared flashing in front of me again: the rocking horse, his capture by the Russians, his return and all the other adventures. Then the light broke in his eyes, my throat was constricted. He did not want to lie down in front of us; it was his way of saying a last farewell. In terrible pain and with his last strength he sent us an unforgettable goodbye. Then he collapsed, Mum caught him in time and together we put him back into bed. Now there was no turning back, his life had been fulfilled. Tears filled my eyes and everything around me was in a blur. The center, the driving force of our lives was gone, on the very same date his mother had died fourteen years earlier.

Dad's body was placed in the provided room next to the Friedberg Mourning Hall. We brought him a large vase with white lilies and put them next to the casket. Every day we went to visit him. My school friend Elisabeth came to his funeral on February 16th and all together we said goodbye to the man we owed so much. To me he was and always will remain a hero.

My father Artur

Postscript

Kapa and I took over the management of the company and we had three children. He was managing director and as from 1967 owner of the Maiwald KG. He brought the company all the way up once again, and employed new staff. He invented more new machines, and built new factory buildings, a spacious showroom and what else was needed. In 1966, he flew to South America to consider an offer managing a tannery and relocate there. At first it looked quite good, but the political situation was too uncertain, and after three months he returned to Germany. We were never discouraged, even when times were bad. I never became a horse owner and rider. Mum still spent a lot of time in the tannery and supported me at home. She loved her grandchildren and let them get away with almost anything. Our children got high school degrees, our son became a Leather Engineer and Master Tanner in the fifth generation. Kapa and Jeron were a good team and it was interesting to see them working together. I know that there was a deep love between them.

My mother Klara in 1995

Mum had to spend the last five years in a wheelchair. She never wanted to be a burden, and she never really accepted it. She always lived in our household until she passed away on December 16th, 1999 just days before her ninety-third birthday. Her bravery and courage is an inspiration to us all and will never be forgotten. We three daughters spent the last days and hours at her side. Missing you always.

Kapa was an energetic man, a benevolent leader and a loving husband. We looked after the family and spent a happy life together. He was my mainstay after Dad's death, our love is everlasting. We travelled to many countries, but our biggest journey together came to an end eventually. He was diagnosed with cancer, and two major surgeries and chemotherapy did not save him. He was taken from us on February 14th, 2005 in Frankfurt and was buried in Friedberg two days later, just a few yards from my parents' grave. My darling, thank you for your love, I miss you! All this happened a hundred years after the birth of my father. After eighty years of existence, and exactly fifty years in Friedberg it was up to me, to take the name "Gerberei und Pelzveredlung Maiwald KG" from the records. The name has gone but will not be forgotten. My working life ends here.

My husband Kaspar in 2003

Ruth stayed in Scherfede. In 1953 she married Heinz Scholle, who was now Master Carpenter and had built a small house in Scherfede where Ruth is still living today. For Ruth the drama was not over. Right in front of her house her first son was run over by a car at the age of six and killed. Her husband Heinz died of a stroke only fifty-six years old and from then on, Ruth carried on alone with three sons, all of which were not working yet. She took over the funeral home of her husband. In the first years after our move, we often visited them; Mum always went there during the school holidays in order to mind the grandchildren.

Ruth and Heinz

Ursula married Erwin K. in Friedberg and had two daughters. The whole family lived in our house until 1965 and then moved into a new house in the neighbourhood. Erwin passed away in October 2013.

My cousin Ruth moved to Fichtelberg, Bavaria, at the age of eighteen, where she had a job lined up. She married Willi Reichenberger and had two sons. Her mother Frieda lived most of the time in Friedberg and then later moved to Fichtelberg. She died last of the Löffel siblings on July 29th, 2005.

The relatives of my parents were spread over East and West Germany, where the ones in the east were worse off. East Germany became a communist country under Russian occupation, the aftermath of the war lingered for decades.

Two of the Schulte brothers, Heinrich and Josef, called Jupp, took over their father's company and expanded. Heribert went independent with his own company in the city of Essen. Josef snr died on October 5th, 1965, and Maria on May 26th, 1972.

My girlfriend Gisel became a teacher and founded her own family with the teacher Siegfried Marquard in Niesky on the Polish border. They had two children and I became godmother to their daughter. The travel conditions were very strict and I could see them only every few years. During the communist era she was not allowed to come to West Germany. Every year we would send each other Christmas presents. Gisel told me that Mr. Kretschmer senior from Heidau was later blacklisted in East Germany because of his sons and died very poor, while his son Otto became a high rank officer of the Federal Marine in West Germany. Our families met in 1972 in the Czech Republic for the first time. After her retirement, we saw each other more often, because the travel restrictions were dropped after the re-unification. My oldest friend died in 2011, and of course I paid her last respects. Thank you, Gisela!

Gisel Just

Aunt Christine died after a stroke at 72 years of age. Two older women arrived from the GDR to attend the funeral. They were relatives of Robert's. He said that one arrived with an empty suitcase she wanted to fill with Christine's clothing. Aunt Christine was a size 16 or 18 whereas the relative was small and skinny. They had lunch and dinner with us and they liked our place. In fact, they were thrilled and would have liked to stay, but Kapa had to take them all back to Frankfurt at night. After Christine's death Kapa sometimes picked up Robert from Frankfurt, who was 76 years old when he died in 1969. Kapa planted conifers on their grave. Uncle Robert died of a skin disease in a nursing home called St. Bardo in Friedberg, where he had spent the last two years. Most of the time he was in bed, but sometimes I pushed him in a wheelchair in a nearby park. Pushing the wheelchair was very hard for me and quite a challenge. I was the last one who saw Robert alive and I was holding his hand when he passed away. Their mutual grave was located at the Friedberg cemetery and was leveled in 1999 after thirty years. The service was held in Frankfurt, because he had friends there, then the funeral took place in Friedberg. Christine and Robert used to be social democrats and politically engaged. Robert had worked for Dad since the times in Glockschütz. He had lost his former job because he was a member of the Socialist Party. From 1933 to 1945 there was only the Nazi party, all other parties were banned. I think he also was in Heidau until he was drafted. He was later captured by the Americans and had to harvest oranges in California. They gave him a metal ring there and when the orange was bigger than the ring, it had to be picked. Back in Germany he got a job at the German Railway, which you could tell by the writing on our tea towels... Aunt Christine had worked for a cleaning company, which had a contract with the Deutsche Bank. Christine actually cleaned the vaults under observation. She had lost all the men in her life except for Robert. To make the tragedy complete, a nephew who was studying in Frankfurt died from cancer even before he could finish university. He was a son of Uncle Robert's brother or sister and after the expulsion from Silesia he had lived near the city of Bochum. He then moved in with the Arlt's in Frankfurt. Aunt and uncle both slept on a sofa bed and the nephew had a bed at the wall, for it was only one room. Robert made me his sole heir and left me five thousand Deutsche Marks. Kapa cleaned up the small apartment after his funeral, so it could be leased again. Most of the furniture was no longer useable and was discarded.

My dear friend Elisabeth Laudage married the tailor Theo Schomacher and left Rimbeck. They had three children and she became the godmother of our youngest daughter. Our friendship continued to her last day and we visited each other regularly. She passed away in September 2013 and just about everybody in the village came to her funeral. I was there with Ursula, Jeron and his wife Nicole. Thanks for everything, Elisabeth.

Ingeborg and Elisabeth 2012

Gerda Dittrich married in Rimbeck and still lives there with her husband Rudi who fought in Italy and was wounded three times. Jeron visited both of them in 2012 for the first time.

Ingeborg and Gerda 2012

Hilda Jungfer was also on our transport. She found a job in the Warburg District as a housekeeper in a good family. She retired late and went to a nursing home in Rimbeck. Kapa and I visited her once and she remembered our adventures as if it was yesterday. She passed away in the early 2000's in Rimbeck.

Our former nanny Angela from the Czech Republic came for some time to Friedberg and minded our children.

Ruth, Ursula with Erwin, Kapa and I travelled together to Heidau in 1998 and visited our former house, which we found almost unchanged. We could still see the bullet holes of the Red Army. The factory chimney was also unchanged, all the factory buildings were dismantled and the bricks were taken to build new homes elsewhere. My old school building was now a family home. Our former fields were not looked after. We all had tears in our eyes, for us women the past came up again. In 2010 I travelled with my son to Breslau, Liegnitz and Heidau, of course. We walked together through the village and I showed him all the important places and buildings, provided they were still there. There were five families living in our old house; the whole yard was overgrown with tall weed. Nothing had been restored or repaired except the roof. Two scruffy little boys were watching us, and we gave each one a chocolate bar. No words were exchanged and they disappeared into the thicket after. This time it was the last farewell, with bitter tears.

The End

Epilogue by the author Jeron North

It took almost four years to write and complete this book. From the very beginning of this journey I saw it as my duty to write it as it happened and always double-check with my mother. For the first time I heard the complete story and I wished I had done it much earlier. I am grateful that I was given the opportunity to understand what my mother and her family went through so many years ago but it seems to me that it was only yesterday. I feel honoured to be a member of this family and my only regret is that I never had the chance to meet my grandfather Artur. I would have loved to grow up in his presence. This book is a love story of a family that never gave up hope although they lost everything.

I believe we can all learn from this and ask more questions and question the answers. We should never be satisfied with a mainstream opinion and mass media propaganda which more or less comes from one source. The first question we must always ask is who makes a profit from it. That is where the answers can be found. Many books have been written about the true background of wars and stock market crashes.

Once the German troops had surrendered, the US moved quickly to commercially exploit all German patents and scientific knowledge. German Chancellor Konrad Adenauer stated later:

'According to a statement made by an American expert, the patents formerly belonging to IG Farben have given the American chemical industry a lead of at least 10 years. The damage thus caused to the German economy is huge and cannot be assessed in figures. It is extraordinarily regrettable that the new German inventions cannot be protected either, because Germany is not a member of the Patent Union. Britain has declared that it will respect German inventions regardless of what the peace treaty may say. But America has refused to issue such a declaration. German inventors are therefore not in a position to exploit their own inventions. This puts a considerable brake on German economic development.'

In 2010 the last payment of the reparation costs of the First World War was made by the German government.

With the invasion of Soviet troops, most of Silesia fell under Polish administration. 3-4 million Silesia Germans fled or were expelled and became ultimately victims to the thorough 'ethnic cleansing.' About 387,000 Germans are considered "war losses," which means they were murdered in the camps, starved to death, killed in the Soviet deportation or missing (Federal Statistical Office 1958). Even the city of Görlitz was divided in 1945; the eastern district now forms the Polish city of Zgorzelec. Only in Upper Silesia still lives a small German minority. There is land west of the Neisse River which is now part of the Free State of Saxony, and thus belongs to Germany.

This little part of Silesia is all that is left on German soil.

The Maiwald family in Breslau 1938

Ingeborg in Breslau 2010

Pauline's handbag

Jeron North (with his father in the background)

This book was finished on February 8th, 2013, exactly 68 years after the dreadful day in Heidau.

I would like to thank my mother Ingeborg for her tremendous work with all my heart. We can only imagine how hard it was for her to take this emotional journey again. Thanks also to my wife Nicole and my friends Peter Boyle and Anna Welsh for their support.

It is my dream to buy the house in Heidau and bring it back to Germany. It shall be a meeting point for refugees and a symbol that they are not forgotten. For donations please use contact email address "readmorebooks101@gmail.com". Thank you so much!

Thanks to everyone for reading this book.

Peace and Friendship.

-JN-

Appendix

The Currency Reform

During the first two years of occupation the occupying powers of France, United Kingdom, United States, and the Soviet Union were not able to successfully negotiate a possible currency reform in Germany. Due to the strains between the Allies each zone was governed independently as regards monetary matters. The US occupation policy was governed by the directive JCS 1067 (in effect until July 1947), which forbade the US military governor 'to take any steps to strengthen German financial structure'. As a consequence a separate monetary reform in the U.S. zone was not possible. Each of the Allies printed its own occupation currency.

Ludwig Erhard introduced the Deutsche Mark on Sunday, June 20, 1948. The old Reichsmark and Rentenmark were exchanged for the new currency at a rate of DM 1 = RM 1 for the essential currency such as wages, payment of rents etc., and DM 1 = RM 10 for the remainder in private non-bank credit balances, with half frozen. Large amounts were exchanged for RM 10 to 65 pfennigs. In addition, each person received a per capita allowance of DM 60 in two parts, the first being DM 40 and the second DM 20.

A few weeks later Erhard, acting against orders, issued an edict abolishing many economic controls which had been originally implemented by the Nazis, and which the Allies had not removed. He did this, as he often confessed, on Sunday because the offices of the American, British, and French occupation authorities were closed that day. He was sure that if he had done it when they were open, they would have countermanded the order.

The introduction of the new currency was intended to protect western Germany from a second wave of hyperinflation and to stop the rampant barter and black market trade (where American cigarettes acted as currency). Although the new currency was initially only distributed in the three western occupation zones outside Berlin, the move angered the Soviet authorities, which regarded it as a threat. The Soviets promptly cut off all road, rail and canal links between the three western zones and West Berlin, starting the Berlin Blockade. In response, the U.S. and Britain launched an airlift of food and coal and distributed the new currency in West Berlin as well.

Since the 1930s, prices and wages had been controlled, but money had been plentiful. That meant that people had accumulated large paper assets, and that official prices and wages did not reflect reality, as the black market dominated the economy and more than half of all transactions were taking place unofficially. The reform replaced the old money with the new Deutsche Mark at the rate of one new per ten old. This wiped out 90% of government and private debt, as well as private savings. Prices were decontrolled, and labour unions agreed to accept a 15% wage increase, despite the 25% rise in prices. The result was the prices of German export products held steady, while profits and earnings from exports soared and were poured back into the economy. The currency reforms were simultaneous with the $1.4 billion in Marshall Plan money coming in from the United States, which primarily was used for investment. In addition, the Marshall plan forced German companies, as well as those in all of Western Europe, to modernize their business practices, and take account of the wider market. Marshall Plan funding overcame bottlenecks in the surging economy caused by remaining controls (which were removed in 1949), and opened up a greatly expanded market for German exports. Overnight, consumer goods appeared in the stores, because they could be sold for realistic prices, emphasizing to Germans that their economy had turned a corner.

In the Soviet occupation zone of Germany (later the German Democratic Republic), the East German mark (also named 'Deutsche Mark' from 1948 to 1964 and colloquially referred to as the Ostmark) was introduced a few days afterwards in the form of Reichsmark and Rentenmark notes with adhesive stamps to stop the flooding in of Reichsmark and Rentenmark notes from the west.

Source: www.wikipedia.org

Made in the USA
Middletown, DE
05 March 2022